CHRISTIAN HEROES: THEN & NOW

JACOB DESHAZER

Forgive Your Enemies

CHRISTIAN HEROES: THEN & NOW

JACOB DESHAZER

Forgive Your Enemies

JANET & GEOFF BENGE

YWAM PUBLISHING

P.O. BOX 55787   SEATTLE, WA 98155

YWAM Publishing is the publishing ministry of Youth With A Mission (YWAM), an international missionary organization of Christians from many denominations dedicated to presenting Jesus Christ to this generation. To this end, YWAM has focused its efforts in three main areas: (1) training and equipping believers for their part in fulfilling the Great Commission (Matthew 28:19), (2) personal evangelism, and (3) mercy ministry (medical and relief work).

For a free catalog of books and materials, call (425) 771-1153 or (800) 922-2143. Visit us online at www.ywampublishing.com.

Jacob DeShazer: Forgive Your Enemies
Copyright © 2009 by YWAM Publishing

Published by YWAM Publishing
a ministry of Youth With A Mission
P.O. Box 55787, Seattle, WA 98155-0787

Library of Congress Cataloging-in-Publication Data
Benge, Janet, 1958–
Jacob Deshazer : forgive your enemies / Janet and Geoff Benge.
    p. cm. — (Christian heroes then & now)
  Includes bibliographical references.
  ISBN 978-1-57658-475-0 (pbk.)
  1. DeShazer, Jacob, 1912–2008—Juvenile literature. 2. World War, 1939–1945—Prisoners and prisons, Japanese—Juvenile literature. 3. World War, 1939–1945—Aerial operations, American—Juvenile literature. 4. World War, 1939–1945—Campaigns—Japan—Juvenile literature. 5. Prisoners of war—Japan—Biography—Juvenile literature. 6. Prisoners of war—United States—Biography—Juvenile literature. 7. Missionaries—United States—Biography—Juvenile literature. 8. Missionaries—Japan—Biography—Juvenile literature. 9. Forgiveness—Religious aspects—Christianity—Juvenile literature. I. Benge, Geoff, 1954– II. Title.
  D805.J3B36 2009
  940.54'2521674092—dc22
  [B]   2009003019

Unless otherwise noted, Scripture quotations are taken from the Revised Standard Version of the Bible, Copyright 1946, 1952, 1971 by the Division of Christian Education of the National Council of the Churches of Christ in the USA. Used by permission. Verses marked KJV are taken from the King James Version of the Bible.

Second printing 2012

Printed in the United States of America

Christian Heroes: Then & Now

Adoniram Judson

Amy Carmichael

Betty Greene

Brother Andrew

Cameron Townsend

Clarence Jones

Corrie ten Boom

Count Zinzendorf

C. S. Lewis

C. T. Studd

David Bussau

David Livingstone

Dietrich Bonhoeffer

D. L. Moody

Elisabeth Elliot

Eric Liddell

Florence Young

George Müller

Gladys Aylward

Hudson Taylor

Ida Scudder

Isobel Kuhn

Jacob DeShazer

Jim Elliot

John Wesley

John Williams

Jonathan Goforth

Lillian Trasher

Loren Cunningham

Lottie Moon

Mary Slessor

Nate Saint

Paul Brand

Rachel Saint

Rowland Bingham

Sundar Singh

Wilfred Grenfell

William Booth

William Carey

*Unit study curriculum guides
are available for select biographies.*

*Available at your local Christian
bookstore or from YWAM Publishing
1-800-922-2143 / www.ywampublishing.com*

East Asia

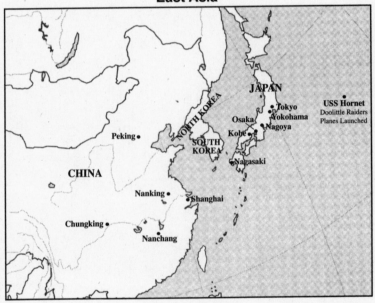

Contents

Chapter 1

Into the Darkness

It was Jake DeShazer's turn to jump. Jake slid his pistol, knife, and packets of rations into the pockets of his leather jacket and edged toward the open hatch. The howl of the wind was deafening, drowning out the drone on the Mitchell B-25 bomber's engines. As he clawed his way along, Jake recalled all that he had been taught during Army Air Corps training about making a parachute jump. At that time the closest he'd come to making a parachute jump was lowering himself through the hatch of a bomber parked on the ground and dropping to the tarmac. But this was no exercise. After thirteen hours aloft, the bomber had empty fuel tanks. The engines would cut out at any moment now. It was time to bail out before the plane crashed.

At three thousand feet above China, Jake knew he would not survive unless he followed his training procedures to the letter. With shaking hands he checked the tension on the harness of his parachute and made sure that the handle of the ripcord swung free. Then, as he gingerly began to lower himself from the hatch, the wind caught his legs, flinging them back against the fuselage of the plane. The force of the wind was so strong that Jake had to use every ounce of strength to get himself all the way through the hatch. "You'll never make it, you're going to die," voices inside his head told him. But Jake pushed forward, squeezing his way out. Then suddenly he slipped free and felt himself falling into the darkness.

As he fell, Jake looked up through pelting rain. He could still make out the outline of the B-25. The light from the plane's open hatch cast an eerie glow as the bomber flew away from him. Jake reached up, felt for the handle of his ripcord, and yanked it with all his might. He heard a slight whooshing sound and then felt an upward jerk. He breathed a deep sigh of relief. His parachute had opened. In the distance above, Jake could hear the now sputtering drone of the bomber's engines trailing away. He was totally on his own, enveloped in darkness.

Jake wished it hadn't had to be this way. They were supposed to land, refuel their plane, and fly on to safety farther inland in China. But things had not gone according to plan. And now somewhere out there his four comrades were also falling through the same dark, stormy night. Jake wondered whether he would see any of them again and, if he did, under what circumstances. As he continued to fall through the darkness, other questions flashed through his mind: Would he land on water? In the top of a tree? In a field surrounded by the rifle-toting enemy soldiers who had heard the plane overhead? He had no idea.

Jake felt totally alone, and more than anything at that moment he wished that it was the farm in Madras, Oregon, he was falling toward. But it wasn't. He was on the other side of the world, falling into an unknown country and an uncertain future. For all he knew, these could be the last minutes of his life. How far it all was from his boyhood growing up in Madras.

Chapter 2

Madras

Eight-year-old Jake DeShazer ran the last hundred yards to the Sunday school room at the back of the Free Methodist Church in Madras, Oregon. He was proud of the shiny buckles on his new bib overalls, and he was eager to show them off to the Sunday school teacher.

Minutes later Jake and his younger brother Glenn were seated side by side in the Sunday school room. Jake looked down at the knees of their new overalls. The knees of the pants were just a single shade of dark blue denim, with no patches on them. "Jacob, Glenn," he heard the Sunday school teacher say.

Jake and Glenn looked up.

"Please remind your mother for next Sunday that boys do not wear bib overalls to church. We try to dress in our best clothes to honor the Lord," the teacher said matter-of-factly.

Jake felt his face turn a deep shade of red, and his neck got hot around the collar of his flannel shirt. He fought back the urge to run away. He managed to sit through the Sunday school session, but he hardly heard a word the teacher said, and he mumbled his way through the singing. All he could think of was the delight he had seen in his mother's eyes when she pulled the two new pairs of bib overalls from the Sears, Roebuck package that arrived in the mail and presented a pair each to Jake and Glenn.

"Look, boys," she had said, "brand-new overalls. Take good care of them. They cost a lot of money."

Jake and Glenn had grinned at each other—Jake because his mother normally sewed his clothes with fabric from his stepfather's worn clothes, and Glenn because he always inherited Jake's hand-me-downs.

Now with Sunday school finally over, Jake's thoughts were in turmoil. Why couldn't the first new clothes he'd ever had be good enough for church—for God? He didn't know. What he did know was that the teacher had made him feel humiliated, and he did not ever want to go back to Sunday school and feel that way again.

Of course, deep in his heart, Jake knew that was not going to be an option. His mother and stepfather, Hulda and Hiram Andrus, were pillars of the Free Methodist Church in Madras. They believed in living the Christian life seven days a week. Every morning after breakfast in their small clapboard farmhouse,

Jake's stepfather would read an entire chapter of the King James Bible, and some of those chapters covered two entire pages of the Bible! All of the children—Jake and Glenn, their older sisters Julia and Ruth, and their half-sister Helen—had to sit quietly and listen to what was being read. Then each person was expected to offer a lengthy prayer of thanks to God for the new day. This was hard to do, especially when Jake knew that the reading of a long chapter would put him and Glenn behind in milking the cow and delivering the milk around town and then would make them late for school.

At school Jake was shy. He did not talk to adults unless he was asked a question. While he liked playing games with the other boys, he found he didn't have much to talk about with them. This was because the DeShazer/Andrus family kept very busy running their small wheat farm. Their life left little room for fun or imagination. From the time he was nine, Jake was expected to handle a team of eight horses, which pulled the combine harvester. Even riding his horse, Minto, had a serious point to it. Jake always carried a rifle with him when he went riding, and he was expected to bring back jackrabbits for dinner.

The only day that the DeShazer/Andrus children had off to play was the Fourth of July, when they were allowed to go swimming along a sandbar in the Deschutes River. If Jake had talked about his family life to his friends at school, he would have discovered that even for life in rural America in the early 1920s, his family had a more rigorous existence than most.

Sometimes Jake's mother told him about his early life in Salem, Oregon. Jake was born in Salem on November 15, 1912, the first son of his mother, Hulda, and his father, Jacob DeShazer. Jake's father had been married before. His first wife had died young, leaving behind four children—a boy and three girls. When Jake's mother married his father, she took on the role of stepmother to his children, giving Jake an older stepbrother and three older stepsisters. Then his mother gave birth to two girls, Julia and Ruth, followed by Jake and Glenn. The family of eight lived simply in Salem. Jacob DeShazer was a lay preacher in the Church of God, which as far as Jake could figure out had meant that his father worked on his small farm during the week and then preached all weekend.

Sadly, Jake's father became ill when Jake was a baby and died from a stomach illness when Jake was only two years old. It was a tragedy for Jake's mother and the eight children she cared for. The family had not only lost a husband and father but also the only way of making ends meet.

Knowing that she could not look after so many children, Jake's mother arranged for the four stepchildren to return to Jake's father's side of the family while she concentrated on feeding and clothing the four children who were her own. This was not an easy time for her or the children. Sometimes food was scarce, the clothes Jake wore were all patched hand-me-downs, and the family never had any money for store-bought gifts or trips.

Three years later, when Jake was five, his mother married Hiram Andrus, a stern, forty-seven-year-old bachelor she had met at a church meeting in Salem. After the wedding the family moved to Hiram Andrus's wheat farm in the small town of Madras, 130 miles east of Salem, just in time for Jake to begin attending school.

In the years that followed, Jake's mother and step-father had another child, Helen, giving Jake a total of one stepbrother, three stepsisters, one half sister, one full brother, and two full sisters. Jake always felt it was a shame that the family had so many girls, because there was so much farm work to be done and he and Glenn had to split the workload between them.

About once a year, the family would take the horse and cart and head to Salem, where they would visit with the other four DeShazer children and attend church camp meetings.

At school Jake liked to play football and baseball, and since he was short and slight, he made a good runner. Despite his love of sports, he could not sign up for the school teams. His stepfather reminded him that work came first—and there was always plenty of work to do on the farm.

Jake survived school. Although he was not an outstanding student, his favorite subject was mathematics, and he harbored hopes of going on to college from high school. However, Jake graduated from high school in 1931, when the United States was in the firm grip of the Great Depression, and there was no money for the family to pay for higher education.

Like many other boys at the time, Jake had to scrap his idea of going to college and look for a job.

Unsure of what else to do, Jake took jobs working on neighboring farms. The work was backbreaking, but Jake was glad to have it. His labor earned him a dollar a day and his board. During this time Jake stopped attending church and participating in the other religious activities he'd had to be a part of when living with his family back on the farm.

Sometimes his half sister Helen would ask him if he believed that Jesus died on the cross. "I guess so," Jake would reply, "but so what? Lots of people died on crosses back then." He could not accept that Jesus was more than a historical figure. He admired his parents' strong faith, but deep down it meant little to him.

Bit by bit, Jake's jobs took him farther and farther from home—and his Christian upbringing. One day he heard about a job opening on the California-Nevada border. Sheepherders from the Basque region of Spain spent their summers grazing sheep in the high mountain meadows of the Sierra Nevada range. In the winter they drove the sheep down to the desert of Nevada. Since the Basque sheepherders were up in the mountains or out on the desert for months at a time, they needed someone to regularly bring them fresh supplies and cook for them.

Jake took the job, and he loved every minute of it. He would begin by buying supplies of beans, flour, and dried fruit for the men, as well as feed for their horses. He would load the supplies onto a pack train of donkeys and guide them on horseback up into the mountains in the summer and the Nevada desert in the winter. Once he located the Basque sheepherders, spread out in separate camps like spokes of a wheel, he would unload the supplies and set up camp. He would then spend his days baking bread in a sage fire and take it, along with other supplies, to the men.

Jake lived an isolated existence, but he loved the endless vista of mountains and desert, the fresh air, and the company of animals. He also liked the money. Since most of the time he was a hundred miles away from the nearest store, he was able to save most of his pay. After two years on the job, in May 1939, Jake had saved up the grand sum of one thousand dollars in the bank. He was ready to go into business for himself.

During his time alone in the high country of California and Nevada, Jake had brought along and read several books on raising turkeys, and he was convinced that he could make money on such a venture. He quit his job supplying the Basque sheepherders, rented a small farm in Butte Falls, Oregon, and bought five hundred turkey chicks.

Keeping the young turkeys alive was a full-time commitment. The birds had to be constantly monitored to make sure they were not too hot or too cold and that they did not get wet. Jake continually adjusted their food intake until they were each gaining about one pound a week. Everything looked good— except for the economy. Instead of the price of turkey meat rising, as it usually did when Thanksgiving approached, the price fell dramatically. When Jake bought the turkey chicks, turkey meat had been fetching twenty-two cents per pound. But twenty-four weeks later, with Thanksgiving approaching, Jake sold the grown turkeys and received only fourteen cents per pound for them.

After settling up his account at the feedlot and paying his rent, Jake was broke. The thousand dollars he had saved, which represented two years of hard work, was gone. Jake was now a single, twenty-seven-year-old man with no money and a high school education. He wanted to settle into some kind of career, but what?

In 1940 Uncle Sam provided the answer. By now war had broken out in Europe, with Great Britain and France facing off against Nazi Germany, which was threatening to overrun the continent. And there was talk of the United States entering the war to assist Britain and France in the fight against Germany. Jake made a practical decision. He knew that if the United States entered the war, single men like him would be the first to be drafted into the military. He decided to sign up ahead of time. That way he could choose the branch of the military he wanted to serve in.

Jake chose the army. He wanted to become a pilot in the Army Air Corps program. He had no problems qualifying for enlistment; he was fit, healthy, and eager to put his brain to work. However, he was disappointed when he was told that he was too old to be a pilot. The army was training only men under the age of twenty-five for that position. Instead, Jake was assigned to the Seventeenth Bombardment Group and sent to newly opened McChord Field, south of Tacoma, Washington, to train as an aircraft mechanic and bombardier.

Jake spent his first year in the army stationed at McChord Field. To his surprise, he liked army life. Not only was he learning important and useful skills, but also he was now receiving a regular paycheck. And there was another thing he liked about army life: for once in his life, Jake had regular time off. Since he had spent most of his life working hard, it felt odd to him at first to be given regular time off with no requirements to do anything else but relax. Before long Jake was reading Westerns at his leisure and going to movies.

As his training time at McChord Field rolled on, Jake wondered when the United States would become involved in the war. Everyone told him that it was inevitable, but it had not yet happened. Jake knew that when the United States did enter the war, he would be ordered overseas to serve—but where?

Chapter 3

Secret Mission

Jake sat on an upturned bucket peeling potatoes and then tossing them into a bowl of cold water. It was December 7, 1941, and there was a chill in the morning air at March Field, just outside Los Angeles. The base was like so many others that Jake had passed through since being assigned to the Army Air Corps Seventeenth Bombardment Group almost two years before.

Jake was enjoying a joke with a fellow potato peeler when the loudspeaker system crackled to life. "Attention," a voice said in a tone that Jake thought more fitting for a funeral than a basewide announcement. "We have just received word that the United States fleet stationed at Pearl Harbor has been attacked by the Japanese. Significant damage and loss of life has been reported. I repeat. We have just received word that the United States fleet stationed at Pearl Harbor has been attacked by the Japanese. Stand by for further information."

Stunned, Jake felt a whole host of emotions rising within him. "Those Japanese are going to pay for this!" he yelled. All around him uniformed men were also shouting. The scene depicted a combination of frustration and anger. The Japanese military, under the control of the emperor, had dared to attack an American fleet in American waters. What would be next?

Over the next several days, more details of the attack and the full damage the Japanese had inflicted at Pearl Harbor were revealed. The attack had come in two waves. The first consisted of 189 Japanese aircraft, followed by another wave of 171 airplanes. When the attack was over, eight American battleships, three destroyers, and three cruisers had been sunk or severely damaged. As well, 188 aircraft were destroyed, 2,403 people had been killed, and another 1,178 were wounded. The Japanese losses during the attack had been minimal: twenty-nine Japanese aircraft had been shot down, five midget submarines had been sunk, and sixty-five Japanese sailors and airmen had been killed or wounded.

In addition, on the same day they attacked Pearl Harbor, the Japanese won battles in the Philippines, Wake Island, Guam, Midway Island, Malaya, Thailand, and Shanghai.

The attacks galvanized the United States into action, and the following day, December 8, 1941, the United States and Britain declared war on Japan. America could no longer claim that the war was "over there in Europe." Japan had delivered war to the country's doorstep.

As the United States entered the Second World War, Jake was not happy with the results as he watched the Japanese gain the upper hand in the Pacific region. Between the attack on Pearl Harbor and New Year's Day 1942, the Japanese bombed Manila and invaded the Philippines. They also seized the island of Guam and invaded Burma, British Borneo, and Hong Kong. The Japanese seemed to be winning every battle they entered and were becoming more emboldened with each passing day.

Millions of Americans agreed with President Franklin D. Roosevelt that something monumental had to be done to stem Japanese aggression. The question was, what? It was impossible to strike Japan itself, since the Japanese occupied all of the land within air-striking distance of their island nation. An aircraft carrier would have to be within three hundred miles of Japan to launch a direct air strike on the country, and there was no way that the Japanese Navy was going to let any American warships get that close.

To make matters even worse, the Germans had launched an offensive against American ships, so that US ships were being attacked in both the Pacific and the Atlantic Oceans. The American public was kept in the dark about most of the German U-boat attacks against civilian ships and their American naval escorts, but word of these attacks filtered through to the men in uniform.

With each enemy attack, Jake grew angrier, and more grateful that he had trained to be both an aircraft mechanic and a bombardier—a direct way for him to make a mark on the war.

By the end of January 1942, Jake had moved on from California. This time he had been assigned to an air base in Columbia, South Carolina. One morning, soon after arriving at his new posting, Jake was checking on a plane's mechanical release arm when a fellow soldier informed him that he was to report to the captain.

As Jake walked across the tarmac, he searched his mind for anything that he had done wrong lately that would cause the captain to want to see him. He'd been to a few bars and dance halls, but he had done nothing out of the usual. He was a shy man and did not attract as much attention as some of the other men. Still, his heart skipped a beat as he stepped into the captain's office.

To Jake's surprise, fifteen or twenty other airmen already were inside the captain's office. Jake inched his way inside the door and scanned the men quickly to see whether he could figure out what they might all have in common, but nothing came to him.

The captain appeared to be waiting for Jake to arrive before he began. "Men, there's no way to lead up to this and no way to put a fine point on it. I have just been informed that we have a very dangerous mission coming up, and we need volunteers." The captain paused and looked around the room. "That's about all I can tell you. As I said, it's volunteers, so if you don't want to step up, that's fine with me."

"Where is the mission going?" one airman asked.

"How long will we be away?" another inquired.

"How many of us are needed?"

"Does this come from the top, or is it a local operation?"

The questions poured out until the captain lifted his hands. "Men, I've told you all I can. In fact, more than that, I've told you all I know. This mission has the highest rating for secrecy that the army gives. You might not know one more thing until you are under way."

Jake stood quietly watching the situation unfold before him.

The men asked a few more questions but got the same answer: the assignment was top secret, and the captain had already told them everything he knew.

"Well, men, let's have a show of hands," the captain concluded. "I'll go around the room, and you raise your hand if you're in."

The captain began with the airman nearest his desk, which meant that Jake would be the last person in the room to be reached. As the captain's eyes fell on each airman in the room, the men raised their hands, until it was Jake's turn. Jake's stomach knotted. He wanted to walk out the door. He did not need to be a hero, not if there was the possibility that it would cost him his life. But every other man in the room had raised his hand, and Jake was too embarrassed to be the only standout. He raised his hand. For better or for worse, he knew that his life was about to be turned upside down.

Within a week the men who had been at the meeting, along with about 120 others, were flying into Eglin Field in the panhandle of Florida. The men still did not know any more about the mission than when they'd volunteered, but it didn't take long before they began to put a few pieces of the puzzle together.

The men were divided into twenty-four crews, each crew consisting of a pilot, a copilot, a navigator, a bombardier, and a gunner/engineer. Jake liked the crew he was assigned to. Even though he was only twenty-nine years old, the other members made him feel like the old man of the group. The next oldest member of the crew was the navigator, twenty-five-year-old Lieutenant George Barr, followed by the twenty-three-year-old pilot, Lieutenant William Farrow; the twenty-two-year-old copilot, Lieutenant Robert Hite; and twenty-year-old Sergeant Harold Spatz, the gunner/engineer. The remainder of the men in the room who had not been assigned to a crew were told that they would be ground personnel for the mission.

On March 3, 1942, the men who had volunteered for the secret mission were called together in a briefing room at Eglin Field. Jake huddled in with the rest of the men. Moments later the door to the briefing room swung open and in strode a short, middle-aged man with a cleft chin and receding hairline. Jake could see that the man wore the insignia of the rank of lieutenant colonel.

The room went quiet as the man walked to the podium at the front. "My name is Doolittle," he said.

So this is the famous Jimmy Doolittle, Jake thought. He had heard much about Doolittle's legendary flying achievements, but this was the first time he had ever seen the man in person. Doolittle had set all kinds of flight speed records, and in 1922 he had set a record flying from Florida to San Diego, California, in twenty-one hours, nineteen minutes, making one stop to refuel in Texas. Doolittle also had pioneered the development and deployment of instruments in aircraft. In 1929 he became the first pilot to take off, fly, and land blind (that is, using only his instruments and not his eyesight to guide him).

"I've been put in charge of the project you men have volunteered for," Doolittle continued. "It's a tough mission and will be the most dangerous thing most of you will have ever done. Any man can drop out now if he wants to, and nothing will ever be said about it."

Nobody in the room took up the colonel's offer to walk away.

Finally, a boyish-looking lieutenant raised his hand. Jimmy Doolittle signaled for the young man to speak.

"Sir, can you give us any more information about the mission?" the lieutenant asked.

"I'm sorry, I can't do that right now," Doolittle replied, shaking his head.

The lieutenant colonel then went on to explain how important secrecy was to the mission. He urged the men not to speculate among themselves as to what the mission might be. And they were to tell no one, not even their wives and girlfriends, about what they were up to. If anyone outside the military got too nosy or asked too many questions about what the men were doing, they were to report the name of that person to their commanding officer so that the FBI could be called in to investigate the person.

Jimmy Doolittle then went on to explain the importance of teamwork on the mission. The five-man crews were to train until they flowed together as a tight, cohesive unit. The pilots were to concentrate on getting their aircraft off the ground in the shortest distance with the heaviest load.

The aircraft the crews would be flying on the mission was the Mitchell B-25 bomber. Each crew was assigned to a bomber and was told they could name the plane if they wanted to. Jake and his crew settled on *Bat Out of Hell* as the name of their plane, while others chose names like *Whirling Dervish* and *Ruptured Duck*.

It did not take long for the crews to notice that all sorts of modifications had been made to their B-25s. These changes provided some clues as to what Special Aviation Project #1, as the secret mission had now been dubbed, might entail. For one, the bombers had extra rubber fuel tanks installed inside them that extended the fuel capacity of the plane from 646 gallons to 1,141 gallons. One of the extra fuel tanks was installed in the bomb bay. As a result, new shackles had been installed in the bomb bay to hold the bombs. The lower gun turret had been removed to make room for another gas tank. As well, some improvements had been made to the aircrafts' remaining gun turrets. To Jake's surprise, two broom handles painted black now protruded from the back of the tail to give the illusion that the plane had more firepower than it actually had. De-icing equipment had also been fitted to the leading edges of the wings and tail surfaces.

The airmen's flight training in the modified B-25s offered more clues to their mission. At a remote airfield the pilots practiced taking off in the shortest distance possible, within the white outline of an aircraft carrier flight deck painted on the runway. Under the tutelage of Lieutenant Hank Miller (a naval aviator who had been brought in from nearby Pensacola Naval Air Station to train the army pilots in the fundamentals of short takeoffs) the pilots were soon getting their fully loaded bombers off the ground in less than five hundred feet. The pilots also practiced flying low over both land and water and then climbing to fifteen hundred feet to drop their bombs. The pilots were told to calibrate their instruments precisely and work out fuel efficient settings for their engines.

Meanwhile, the rest of the men on the crew learned how to perform the duties of the other members of the crew so that they could take over if something happened to one of the crewmen on the mission.

During the training period, two of the bombers and their crews were eliminated from the mission because of poor performance, leaving the total number of planes and crews for the mission at twenty-two.

Throughout this time the men, including Jake, couldn't resist trying to speculate as to what their secret mission might be. The Germans were continuing their onslaught against Allied merchant and naval ships in the Atlantic Ocean. Some men thought that their secret mission might be to help France get stranded airplanes off the Caribbean island of Martinique. Still others speculated that they might be dispatched to protect the Panama Canal or to patrol the Aleutian Islands off the west coast of Alaska. It was all speculation. Yet the men knew that it was only a matter of time before they would learn the specifics of the mission they had volunteered for.

Then on the morning of March 23, 1942, three and a half months after the United States had declared war on Japan, Lieutenant Colonel Jimmy Doolittle addressed the men. "Today's the day we move out," he began. "We are headed for McClellan Field, outside of Sacramento, California, to be exact. File your flight plans. I'll see you there."

Chapter 4

"This Ship Is Bound for Tokyo"

The flight from Florida to the West Coast was a dream come true for many of the Army Air Corps pilots. The men had been instructed to practice their low-level flying, or hedgehopping, as it was called, on the flight out. Jake spent the two days of flying strapped into the bombardier's position in the Plexiglas-enclosed nose of the airplane. He whooped with exhilaration at his first-class view as the B-25 bomber skimmed along just feet above the ground. And he laughed uproariously as cows in Texas and New Mexico fled as the plane buzzed inches above their heads.

The first day's flying took them to Kelly Field in San Antonio, where they spent the night when the weather turned foul. The following day they took to the air again and completed their journey to McClellan Field in California. All twenty-two of the bombers made it safely to their destination. That night the men huddled into the mess hall at McClellan Field to await further instruction. They soon learned that they were to make the short trip from the Sacramento Valley to Alameda Naval Air Station, just outside of San Francisco. The airmen of Special Aviation Project #1 quickly concluded that their planes were to be loaded aboard a ship bound for somewhere in the Pacific region.

Before they left for Alameda Naval Air Station, the planes were given one last inspection. The men also learned that only sixteen of the twenty-two bombers would be going on the mission.

On April 1, 1942, the planes were back in the air headed for Alameda Naval Air Station. In a last fit of free-spirited flying, some of the pilots flew their aircraft under the Golden Gate Bridge en route, though Jake's pilot, Will Farrow, exercised a little more caution. Jake was mesmerized by his first glimpse of San Francisco from the air. Peering through the panes of Plexiglas, he could see gray battleships lined up in the harbor. He could also see the Golden Gate Bridge that spanned the entrance to the bay, Alcatraz Prison set on a rocky island in the middle of San Francisco Bay, and the concrete and wood buildings of the city huddled over the hills. As the plane made its final approach into Alameda, it flew directly over an aircraft carrier.

"There are three of our planes on the deck," the navigator, George Barr, announced over the intercom in his Brooklyn accent.

Sure enough, Jake looked down and saw three of the Mitchell B-25s lined up on the deck of the carrier. He was puzzled, though. Sailors appeared to be tying them down on the deck. Normally, B-25s had their wings unbolted and taken off and were stored below deck when they were transported, leaving the aircraft carrier's fighter planes on deck. Everyone knew that B-25s were useless at sea. The bombers could not take off from an aircraft carrier, since the ship's flight deck was designed to accommodate small fighter aircraft. Jake wondered why an aircraft carrier would give up deck space for its own planes in order to accommodate Army Air Corps bombers.

Jake had not solved the puzzle when Will brought their bomber in for a smooth landing at Alameda Naval Air Station. Lieutenant Colonel Jimmy Doolittle met the plane as it taxied to a halt.

"Hello, boys. Glad you made it. Any problems with your plane?" Doolittle asked. "Any malfunctions or concerns?"

"No, Sir. She flew like a charm," gunner/engineer Harry Spatz replied.

Doolittle smiled. "Very good. Taxi down the ramp and get her loaded up," he said, pointing in the direction of the pier, where the aircraft carrier they had flown over was tied up.

Jake and the crew of the *Bat* breathed a sigh of relief—their plane would be going on the mission.

After taxiing to the dock, Will cut the bomber's engines. When the crew had clambered out of the plane, sailors began swarming over the aircraft. They drained the remaining fuel from the fuel tanks and then towed the plane down the pier to the side of the aircraft carrier.

Jake marveled at the size of the carrier. She was the USS *Hornet,* and she was massive. Her flight deck was 909 feet long and 127 feet wide, and the vessel towered over everything around her. Jake craned his neck to take in the sight. Along the ship's side, just below the flight deck, he could see her 20-millimeter and 1.1-inch guns. Her hull was painted in a camouflage pattern of streaks of navy blue and dark and light grays. This pattern was supposed to make it more difficult for enemy aircraft and ships to see and target the vessel.

Jake and the other members of his crew remained dockside until their bomber was safely aboard the aircraft carrier. A large crane was used to lift the plane off the dock and set it down on the *Hornet*'s decks, where sailors chocked the plane's wheels and lashed the plane down to the deck. The *Bat* was the last of the sixteen bombers to be loaded, and the plane's tail hung over the rear of the *Hornet*'s flight deck.

Once the plane was safely aboard, the crew of the *Bat* boarded the USS *Hornet*. When all the Army Air Corps bombers and their crews were aboard ship, tugboats pulled alongside the *Hornet*, pulling it away from the dock. But they did not sail far. They simply crossed the bay and dropped anchor off San Francisco.

That night the crew members of the B-25 bombers were allowed a night of shore leave in the city. As Jake wandered the streets of San Francisco, he wondered whether this would be the last time he ever set foot in the United States. He recalled a phrase that Jimmy Doolittle had thrown out in a casual moment during a briefing that morning. "Think of it this way, boys. Some of you will be coming back here as heroes and some of you as angels." Given that Jake did not believe in angels, he certainly hoped that he would be returning home in some earthly form.

The following morning, April 2, 1942, the USS *Hornet* weighed anchor and set sail on the mission. Accompanying the *Hornet* on this unknown mission were the cruisers *Vincennes* and *Nashville*; the destroyers *Gwin*, *Grayson*, *Meredith*, and *Monssen*; and the oiler *Cimarron*. Jake stood on deck with the other airmen as they set sail, hoping to get one last glimpse of their homeland. However, a heavy fog socked in the city and San Francisco Bay, and the men could barely make out the girders of the Golden Gate Bridge as they passed beneath it.

A single, unspoken question hung in the air: Where was this ship taking them?

The men did not have to wait long to find out. The USS *Hornet* and her escorts were only ten miles out to sea when the crews of the B-25 bombers were summoned to a briefing.

When the men had all assembled in the wardroom, Jimmy Doolittle matter-of-factly explained the mission to them. They were on their way to Japan. When they were four hundred miles off the coast of Japan, the crews would take off in their bombers from the deck of the *Hornet* and fly over Japan, bombing the cities of Tokyo, Yokohama, Nagoya, and Kobe. After the bombing, the crews were to fly on to China and land their airplanes at the city of Chuchow, some two hundred miles south of Shanghai. There they would refuel their planes and fly on to Chungking, China. While the Mitchell B-25 bombers could take off from the deck of the *Hornet*, it would be impossible for them to return and land on the deck of the carrier.

"If any of you don't want to go, tell me now, because the chances of your making it back are pretty slim," Doolittle told the men.

Nobody said a word.

When he heard the mission outlined, Jake felt scared. They were about to undertake a dangerous mission that could easily get them all killed. Yet he marveled at the audacity of the plan. A part of Jake was exhilarated because the Japanese were finally going to be paid back for the Pearl Harbor attack— and he was going to be a part of the action!

Jake joined his fellow crewmen as they walked the flight deck of the USS *Hornet*. The men were seeing that deck through new eyes. The deck was now a heaving, twisting runway surrounded by a churning gray ocean. As the men walked, each one was alone with his own thoughts. Jake was confident that Will Farrow and copilot Bob Hite would give it their best shot, but he was also painfully aware that they were the youngest and least experienced crew of the sixteen who would be flying out over Japan. After some quick math, Jake worked out his crew's average age to be only twenty-three and a half years.

The rest of the day passed quietly. The army and navy had a long-standing rivalry, and Jake and the other Army Air Corps men were very much aware of tension between them and their begrudging navy hosts. The B-25 crewmen were crammed into fore-cabins on the *Hornet* with old, lumpy mattresses and bed frames that squeaked every time the ship heaved. And being so far forward seemed to magnify every heave and roll the ship made as she plowed her way forward.

That night, just as the men were getting ready for dinner, a Klaxon horn began to blast and a voice over the loudspeakers howled, "Man your battle stations!" Suddenly, the twenty-two hundred crewmen of the *Hornet* exploded into action, with sailors running in all directions. Jake and the other Army Air Corps men made their way up to the flight deck and climbed into their bombers.

By now Jake was aware that this was just a drill, but nonetheless, all around him the chaos continued. He watched as men, all in color-coordinated shirts, swarmed the planes. The sailors in blue shirts stood by to unlash each plane and push out the chocks that kept the wheels in place. The sailors in red shirts loaded bombs into the bomb bays of the aircraft, while the sailors in yellow shirts worked with the pilots as they ran through their final checks and then stood ready to direct the planes into take-off formation.

The gunners were using the practice run to test their guns, and lines of red explosions lit up the evening sky. Several of the other vessels in the escort fleet were also manning their battle stations, adding to the noise, the bursts of bright light, and the acrid smell of gunpowder that drifted back across to the *Hornet*'s flight deck.

For Jake, this was an entirely new look at war. Up until this time he had been serving on land, far from conflict. Now, as his heart raced, he got the feel of what it would be like to be in an actual battle on a floating target. As he watched the drill proceed, he wondered just how far west Japanese submarines and gunboats patrolled. Every week it seemed like they were gaining the upper hand. Just four weeks ago, on March 1, 1942, the Japanese had defeated a combined US Navy and Allied fleet in the Battle of the Java Sea and seized control of the Dutch East Indies (Indonesia).

Jake thought of the details that were just beginning to filter out about the cruel treatment of captured soldiers in the Philippines by the Japanese after they had overrun that country. On the island of Luzon, seventy-five captured American and Filipino prisoners of war were being moved from the Bataan Peninsula sixty miles north to prison camps near San Fernando. The Japanese refused to give the captured soldiers food or water as they marched. Those who were too weak to keep marching were tortured mercilessly by Japanese soldiers. No one knew for sure how many captured soldiers had been killed by their captors, but word had it that the route they followed was strewn with dead bodies after the Japanese and their captives had passed by. As a result, the Allies were quickly coming to the conclusion that when it came to prisoners of war, the Japanese were a much more ruthless and inhumane enemy than the Germans, whom they were fighting in Europe and North Africa, and that it was a horrible fate for a soldier to fall into the hands of the Japanese.

Colonel Doolittle briefed the men to leave behind all pictures, personal identification, orders, letters, diaries, and anything else that might link them to the *Hornet*, their units back in the United States, and the places where they had trained for the mission. Then, if they were captured by the Japanese, the enemy would not be able to trace them. The navy would mail all their personal belongings back to their homes in the United States.

Two days after the USS *Hornet* set sail from San Francisco, the ship's master, Captain Marc Mitscher, made a shipwide announcement over the loudspeaker. "This ship is bound for Tokyo," he said. "We will carry the army bombers to the coast of Japan for the bombing of Tokyo."

There was total silence, and then a huge cheer went up as sailors began to jump up and down with glee. Jake, who was on deck, watched as the signalmen used their semaphore flags to signal the news to the escort ships. Soon cheers were carried on the wind from those ships as well. One of the sailors aboard the *Hornet* started singing aloud, "Heigh-ho.

Heigh-ho. We're off to Tokyo. We'll bomb and blast and come back fast. Heigh-ho. Heigh-ho."

Following the announcement of the mission, Jake and the other crew members of the B-25s noticed an immediate turnaround in respect from the *Hornet's* crew. They were served first at mealtime, their rooms were upgraded, and the cooks made their favorite desserts for dinner.

On the evening of Captain Mitscher's announcement, Jake stood alone on deck. Everyone had calmed down a little, and he had had more than enough time to think about the mission ahead. He felt alone and as if his childhood on the farm in Oregon were now a million miles away. He distracted himself by looking at the albatrosses as they wheeled and dipped over the ship. The birds appeared tireless, flying overhead with little effort. Jake watched their tail feathers turn like the rudder of a plane, and he thought of himself up there soon in a Plexiglas cone at the nose of a bomber, part of the first direct attack on one of the most powerful military powers on earth.

Jimmy Doolittle told the men honestly that he gave the mission a 50 percent chance of success. Goose bumps rose on Jake's arms as he contemplated his own odds of ever getting home again, and he did not sleep well that night. But the following day and the next few days were busier than ever. The men were given lectures and demonstrations on first aid. The pilots and navigators received instruction from the *Hornet's* navigator, Commander Frank Akers. Meanwhile, the gunner/engineers divided their time between target practice (shooting at kites flown off the back of the *Hornet)* and tinkering with the bombers in their care. The men were introduced to Lieutenant Commander Stephen Jurika, who had served as an American naval attaché in Japan. Commander Jurika taught the men as much about Asia as he could in the allotted time. The men were soon referring to his lectures as "How to Make Friends and Influence Japanese."

"Memorize this phrase: *lushu hoo megwa fugi,* Chinese for 'I am an American,'" the lieutenant commander instructed the men. He also told of one way to distinguish a Chinese person from a Japanese person. "Look at their feet," he said. "The Chinese have all their toes together while the Japanese have the big toe separated from the others because of years of wearing a thong between them."

One day when Jake was up on deck, a navy oil tanker pulled alongside to refuel the USS *Hornet.* Jake watched as a large, flexible hose was hauled between the two ships and then fuel was pumped through it from the tanker into the *Hornet*'s fuel tanks. It was a particularly rough day, and as the aircraft carrier was refueled, waves broke over the tanker. Suddenly, one particularly large wave caused the bow of the tanker to plunge beneath the surface, causing one of the sailors near her bow to be washed overboard. The "man overboard" alarm was quickly sounded, and the sailor was soon spotted floating in his life vest. A rubber raft was thrown to him from the tanker. The sailor clambered into the raft, and soon a destroyer swooped in to pick him up. A short while later an announcement was made that the sailor had been uninjured. Jake marveled at the sight. People said flying bombers was dangerous work, but so was refueling ships at sea.

The routine of shipboard life was broken with an Easter service on April 5. Many of the Army Air Corps men made a special effort to attend the service, but Jake would not go. It would have made him feel like a hypocrite. He had left his childhood religion totally behind him when he joined the army, and he was not about to go running back to it just because he had a one-way ticket to Tokyo.

Eight days later, on April 13, 1942, the aircraft carrier USS *Enterprise* and seven escort vessels rendezvoused with the USS *Hornet* and her escorts. Now sixteen ships were headed toward Tokyo, one ship for each B-25 hoping to take off for Japan. The USS *Enterprise* was under the command of Admiral William Halsey, who took command of the combined task force headed for Japan.

On April 17, Captain Mitscher announced over the *Hornet*'s loudspeaker system that he wanted all of the B-25 crews to assemble on the flight deck. When they had assembled, Jake listened as the captain made a short speech: "Secretary of the Navy Frank Knox has asked me to return these to Japan." He held up three medals that had been awarded to navy-enlisted men by Japan in 1908. He then handed the medals to Lieutenant Colonel Doolittle. Doolittle took the medals, walked over to a five-hundred-pound bomb that had been brought up on deck for the occasion, and attached them to the bomb.

"Send this one too," Lieutenant Commander Stephen Jurika said, adding the medal he had received from the Japanese in 1940 to the other three medals on the bomb. (He had received this medal while still a naval attaché in Tokyo.)

A cheer went up from the men, and several stepped forward to scrawl slogans on the bomb. One read, "You'll get a BANG out of this!" and another said, "I don't want to set the world on fire—just Tokyo!"

As the medal ceremony drew to a close, Jimmy Doolittle stepped forward and announced, "Men, get your equipment packed. Make final inspections of your planes. It looks like we might be taking off tomorrow instead of the nineteenth. Remember, don't take any personal things with you that would help the Japanese identify you. Anything you leave onboard will be mailed back to your home. Of course, you can still drop out if you want—no questions asked."

The pronouncement hung in the air. Thirty seconds passed, then a minute. No one spoke. Doolittle broke the silence. "Oh, and when we get to Chungking, I'm going to throw you all a party!" he announced.

A cheer went up from the men; the moment of introspection was over. Jake and the other seventy-nine airmen on the mission had a job to do, and there was no turning back now. Tomorrow or the next day they would be flying their bombers directly toward the Empire of the Rising Sun.

Chapter 5

Airborne

Jake sat on the edge of his bunk. It had been a long night. Somewhere around 3:15 AM the ship's general quarters alarm bells had gone off, and everyone, including the Army Air Corps men, had to man his battle station. Nothing happened, and little was said about the incident, but Jake and the others wondered whether possibly a Japanese ship or submarine had spotted them.

It was time to finish packing. Jake slung his B-4 bag out from beneath his bunk and emptied its contents: a navy issue gas mask, a .45-caliber automatic pistol and ammunition clips, a hunting knife like the one he'd used as a kid back in Oregon, a first aid kit, a canteen, a compass, a flashlight, emergency rations, and a life jacket. As he repacked the items, Jake wondered which of them he might need and when. Bailing out over the ocean would require the life jacket, while bailing out over the jungle would require the flashlight and the knife. But since the future was unknowable, Jake would have to wait and see what items, if any, he would need from the bag.

Suddenly, the *Hornet's* Klaxon sounded, followed by the announcement over the loudspeaker: "Army pilots, man your planes!"

Jake stuffed the compass and flashlight back into the bag, grabbed his hat, and headed for the exit. This was a surprise to him and the other bomber crew members, who had expected to be leaving in the afternoon so that they could bomb their targets in Japan at night. Leaving this early meant that they would be making their bombing runs in broad daylight.

Amid the mayhem on the flight deck, Jimmy Doolittle gathered the men and explained that the task force had been spotted by Japanese picketboats and the *Hornet's* radio officer had intercepted a message sent from one of the Japanese boats to Tokyo warning of the presence of American ships. As a result, Admiral Halsey had given the order for the army bombers to take off on their mission before enemy aircraft began swooping in to attack the ships. Jake's heart sank when he heard that they were leaving on the mission two hundred miles short of the planned position. The extra miles would tax the B-25s' fuel supply and give them less opportunity to fly deep into China if necessary. Doolittle wished the men good luck, and then the crews headed to their bombers.

Doc White, a medical doctor and the gunner/ engineer on plane #15, was in charge of the medical needs of the B-25 crews, and he ran to each plane handing out two bottles of alcohol to each man. "This is for cuts and scrapes," he yelled over the roar of the wind.

Jake smiled to himself. Doc White had the good sense to leave giving out the alcohol to the last moment. If the men had received it earlier, they most likely would have drunk it while they played poker at night. Another crew member ran from plane to plane handing out bags of sandwiches to sustain the men on their twelve-hour flight.

The *Bat* was so close to the edge of the *Hornet*'s flight deck that its tail hung out over the stern. As a result, there was no way to fully load the plane, as the back hatch was over the water. Jake threw his bag in through the front hatch and then went around to the other side of the aircraft, where Harry Spatz was amassing extra five-gallon cans of gas for the flight. "Since we have to go farther than anticipated, we need all the gas we can take," Harry told Jake. "And we have to punch holes in the cans before we ditch them. They can't be left afloat to leave a trail back here." Jake understood why Harry's voice had a worried tone. The bombers were now going to have to fly farther than anticipated on their ration of gas if they were to reach China.

Meanwhile, Jake kept busy helping to arm and load bombs into the bomb bays of the B-25 bombers. As he worked away, he could not help but think that they were over six hundred miles from land—Japanese land—two hundred miles more than they had expected to be at takeoff. If they accomplished their mission, they had little chance of getting out alive—or of not being captured by the Japanese. Some of the men had discussed this among themselves on the sea voyage, and the poll was about fifty-fifty between those who would rather be caught by the Japanese and those who would prefer being killed outright.

The flight deck of the USS *Hornet* was a hive of frenzied activity. While bombs were being loaded into the bombers, other navy crewmen were topping off the planes' fuel tanks, shaking the aircraft as they did so to make sure that no air bubbles were in the system that would preclude the maximum amount of gas being loaded into the planes. Meanwhile, mechanics removed the canvas covers that had been placed over the engines to protect them from salt spray during the voyage.

While all of this activity was going on, rain and salt spray washed across the aircraft carrier's deck. As day broke, the weather had turned sour. Bruised purple clouds hung low above the task force, a stiff wind howled across the deck, and thirty-foot waves had the carrier pitching and rolling. Despite the conditions, everyone on deck worked hard and fast to ready the Mitchell B-25s for flight.

"The old man's about to go!" Will Farrow shouted. Jake followed Will's pointed finger to the very first bomber on the *Hornet*'s deck. This was Jimmy Doolittle's plane, and all eyes were on it. Although the pilots had trained for short takeoffs back in Florida, they had done so on dry land. No one had actually ever flown a B-25 bomber off the deck of an aircraft carrier before, and certainly not off a carrier whose flight deck was rising and falling as it rode over mountainous waves. This was the moment of truth, the moment when they would find out whether it was indeed possible to do so. Would Jimmy Doolittle get his bomber airborne, or would he crash over the front of the flight deck into the roiling sea?

The USS *Hornet* was now cruising at full speed into the wind, her bow rising and falling as she rode over the massive waves. Jake watched as Lieutenant Colonel Doolittle cranked the B-25's engines to life. Doolittle let the engines warm up for a few minutes, and then the deck-launching officer, standing to the side of the flight deck ahead of the bomber, began to rotate a checkered flag above his head. The engines of Doolittle's bomber roared to full throttle. As the bow of the *Hornet* began to drop, a deck handler pulled the chocks out from under the wheels, and the deck-launching officer gave the signal for the plane to take off before he dropped facedown on the deck as the wing passed over his head. The nose and left wheels of Doolittle's bomber stayed right on the two white lines painted along the port side of the flight deck. These lines were guides for the pilots. If the pilots kept their wheels on the lines during takeoff, then their right wing would clear the *Hornet*'s command and control island on the starboard side of the ship by six feet.

As the bomber lurched forward, everyone held his breath. Jimmy Doolittle now had 467 feet of flight deck space in which to get his plane into the air. Could he do it?

The *Hornet*'s bow continued to fall, until it looked like Doolittle and his crew were going to fly right into the ocean, and then it began to rise. As it did so, the B-25 lifted off the deck at 8:15 AM, with yards of runway to spare. A huge cheer went up from the deck of the *Hornet*. Mitchell B-25 bombers could take off from the deck of an aircraft carrier.

As Doolittle's plane lifted off the deck, Jake looked up to the ship's island, where Hollywood movie director John Ford and his crew of cameramen were capturing the whole event on film for the navy.

Once he was airborne, Doolittle banked his plane around and made a low pass straight above the *Hornet*'s flight deck. He did this so that his navigator could calibrate the aircraft's navigation system with the aircraft carrier's compass heading. After his pass over the *Hornet*'s deck, Doolittle set course for Tokyo, over eight hundred miles away, and his B-25 was soon swallowed up by the fog and low clouds that hung over the launch area.

As soon as Doolittle's plane had left the deck, a mechanical "donkey" pulled the next B-25 into take-off position. The bomber's engines began to rev up to full speed, and five minutes after Doolittle's plane had taken off, the next bomber was airborne. This plane also overflew the flight deck to calibrate its navigational system, and was then on its way to Japan.

Jake and the other four members of his crew watched as B-25 bomber after B-25 bomber lifted off safely from the deck of the *Hornet*. Finally it was time for them to prepare for takeoff.

Will Farrow, Bob Hite, and George Barr climbed into their positions in the plane, and Will cranked the engines to life. The aircraft's tail still hung out over the stern of the ship, and the plane needed to move forward so that Jake and Harold could load the rest of their gear onto the plane and Harold could take his position in the rear.

Jake watched as the flag was waved for Will to taxi forward into the final loading and takeoff position. Suddenly a gust of wind whipped under the airplane and lifted the plane's nose off the ground. Shouts went up from the sailors on deck as they ran forward with ropes. The men managed to secure the ropes to the plane's nose hooks, but the ropes snapped under the strain. Jake then ran forward and grabbed one of the front-wheel struts. Sailors quickly joined him, and with grim determination they stopped the bomber from sliding overboard with three of her crew inside.

The plane stabilized, and the men backed away. Will gunned the engine as Jake pulled the chocks out from under the wheels. The plane lurched forward. As Jake turned and threw the last few items into the rear hatch of the plane, where Harold was now seated, a spurt of blood splattered across the deck in front of him. He looked up to see a sailor lying under the propeller, his left arm dangling by a thread of skin.

"He backed into the propeller," one of the sailors yelled as Jake ran and knelt down to help the man. The injured sailor looked Jake in the eyes and said to him, "Go get them for me!"

Jake nodded as he helped two sailors carry the injured man out of harm's way.

Jake took a deep breath. Blood was splattered on his uniform, and his heart was heavy. Was he looking at the first death caused by the Doolittle Raid? He didn't know whether the injured sailor would make it, but he had to put the incident out of his mind and get going.

With the last few items loaded into the rear of the plane, Jake scrambled through the front hatch. As he climbed into his position at the front of the plane, his heart sank. The Plexiglas nose cone in front of him had a jagged hole the size of a dinner plate smashed in it, and gale force winds were swirling around inside the cone. Jake concluded that the Plexiglas nose must have bumped into the tail of plane #15 when the wind caused the nose to rear up.

A million thoughts ran through his head as Jake pondered the problem. Of course, he should inform the pilot that the plane was damaged. But what would happen then? They were under strict instructions to report any mechanical failures, with the understanding that any plane that was not fit to fly was to be pushed overboard. But what about a structural problem? The increased drag from the jagged hole would cut into fuel efficiency and the number of miles they could fly, but it wouldn't stop the plane from flying.

As Jake thought about what to do, Will gunned the engines, and Jake felt the B-25 vibrate violently under him. They were preparing for takeoff. Jake buckled himself in. It was too late to do anything about the problem now.

The *Bat*'s engines roared so loudly that Jake thought they were about to tear themselves apart. Then all off a sudden the plane lurched forward and gathered speed. As they raced down the *Hornet*'s flight deck, all Jake could see at the end of the deck was swirling ocean. Then suddenly the ship's bow began to rise, and with a thump, the *Bat* was airborne.

Will banked the B-25 around and flew over the length of the *Hornet*'s flight deck while navigator George Barr calibrated his instruments. Jake glanced at his watch. It was 9:16 AM. It had taken an hour to get all sixteen B-25 bombers airborne.

As they climbed up and away from the USS *Hornet*, Jake looked back. The carrier's flight deck was a hive of activity. Sailors were working the elevators to get their own airplanes up from the hangar below, and all of the ships were turning sharply to the southeast, away from the immediate threat of Japanese attack.

Jake took a deep breath. The first part of the mission—getting airborne—was over. Now it was time to tell Will about the hole in the nose. Jake picked up the intercom that connected him with the pilot and shouted into it. Will sounded concerned and immediately sent copilot Bob Hite down to see what could be done. The wind was roaring so loudly through the hole that the two men were forced to use hand gestures to work on a solution to the problem. Bob and Jake stuffed the hole with a thick coat, but the force of the wind pushed it right back in their faces. After several failed attempts, the men looked at each other and shook their heads. It was obvious that there was no way to plug up the hole while they were flying. Bob headed back to the cockpit to inform Will.

The plane soon settled in to its gas-saving mode, skimming along less than a hundred feet above the ocean. For a moment Jake was back in the United States, hedgehopping over ranch land, scaring the cows below, and whisking the hats off people. That had been fun. This time it was a life-or-death situation.

The flight seemed to go on forever, partly because the extra drag on the plane from the hole in the nose slowed down the *Bat*—a fact that created its own set of worries—but also because the pilots had been instructed to fly slowly, between 150 and 166 miles per hour, to get the maximum gas mileage. If they went any slower they would fall out of the sky.

Not much conversation took place between the five crew members on the flight. The din of engines and the howl of the wind blowing into the plane made it almost impossible to talk without yelling, even over the intercom. Jake made sure that the .30-caliber machine gun in front of him was cocked and loaded and ready to fire and that it slid and turned freely on its mount. He checked and rechecked his bombsight to make sure it was working properly. And he crawled back to the bomb bay to make sure that the bombs were armed and that they would release properly when the time came to drop them over Japan. While doing this, Jake watched Harold in the rear pour gas from the five-gallon cans into the plane's fuel tank. When Harold had done so, he punched holes in the empty cans and threw them out of the aircraft. The holes in the cans would ensure that the cans filled with water and sank, instead of leaving a floating trail on the surface of the water for the Japanese to follow. But mostly the hours passed tediously as the men waited for the coast of Japan to come into view.

Of course, there was plenty for the men to be concerned about. The bomber was bound for the city of Nagoya to drop its bombs. But because of the hole in the Plexiglas, the men wondered if they would arrive over Nagoya a lot later than the other planes, and if the Japanese would be waiting for them. The element of surprise would be taken away. They had no way of knowing how the other planes were faring, and any form of radio contact was out of the question since the signal could be intercepted by the Japanese. Instead, the crew listened in to a Tokyo radio station and watched for signs of life above and below them as the *Bat* wound its way toward Japan.

Chapter 6

Bailout

It was exactly one in the afternoon when the *Bat* reached the Japanese island of Honshu. Navigator George Barr ran his hands over a succession of maps trying to locate the exact spot of coastline they were about to fly over. When he had ascertained their position, he relayed instructions to Will, and the B-25 began banking to the south.

The city of Nagoya, their target, was located about three hundred miles southwest of Tokyo. To reach it, the bomber began to climb up to about seven thousand feet in altitude to cross a range of mountains. As the plane climbed through a bank of clouds, Jake was surprised to see people living high on the mountains. The plane was flying close enough to the mountains that from his perch in the nose of the bomber Jake could see people on the ground. When they saw the plane pass overhead, the people stopped and waved. Jake could clearly make out the faces of children. He chuckled when an old man with a gray beard threw his walking stick to one side and dived to the ground as the plane flew over him. Obviously the people below thought that the plane was one of their own Japanese bombers. Jake fervently hoped that they would drop their load of bombs in Nagoya and be out of harm's way before anyone realized the truth—that they were Americans.

As they crossed the mountains, the weather on the other side was sunny, and the *Bat* basked in the bright Saturday afternoon as it began to descend and close in on Nagoya. As Jake looked down, he frowned. The terrain below did not look much like the maps they had spent so many hours poring over on the USS *Hornet*. Still, Jake trusted that George knew how to do his job and get them to their bombing targets.

Within minutes George's voice came on the intercom. "Get ready to drop bombs at five hundred feet. I see the target," George told Jake. Jake looked out the front of the nose, and there was their first target, a group of oil storage tanks.

The plane continued its steady pace as Jake lined up the target in his bombsight. As they passed over the storage tanks, he pulled the release and dropped two of the five-hundred-pound incendiary bombs from the plane's bomb bay.

After the bombing run, Will banked the B-25 in a turn, and Jake craned his neck to look back and see the damage the bombs had done. The oil storage tanks were in flames, though they hadn't yet exploded. Jake expected to see a massive fireball erupt at any moment. He could see smoke and flames rising from two other locations in the city, and he knew this could mean only one thing—planes #14 and #15 had also made it to Nagoya and dropped their bombs. As they climbed to line up on their next target, Jake could see plane #14 off to the right below them. The *Bat* had made better time than he'd thought on the flight from the *Hornet*. Antiaircraft fire filled the air near plane #14, which was headed south and flying away from Nagoya as fast as it could.

Antiaircraft fire was now also being fired at the *Bat* as it lined up on the next target. Jake soon realized that the smell of acrid smoke that had invaded the plane was not from the burning fuel tanks but from the shots being fired at them from the ground.

Will brought the B-25 around and flew the length of a long low industrial building below. The building was an aircraft factory, and as they flew over it, Jake released the last of the incendiary bombs, which crashed through the roof of the building and exploded in sheets of flame.

With their targets hit, it was time to leave. Will banked the plane sharply as they turned to the south and prepared to follow planes #14 and #15 away from Japan and out over the ocean.

Soon they were skimming low over water as they fled from Nagoya. Jake manned the .30-caliber machine gun in front of him. A small fishing boat loomed on the bay below, bobbing in the calm water. A fisherman, unaware of what had just happened on land, waved at the oncoming plane. Jake, trigger-happy to return fire at someone, fired off several rounds from the machine gun at the fishing boat. He wasn't a good shot, and the bullets missed the boat as the man stopped waving and dived for cover.

Jake laughed as he fired, as much out of relief as anything else. The men had completed their mission. They had dropped their bombs on the right targets and evaded enemy antiaircraft fire. Yet Jake, like the other members of the crew, knew the worst was still ahead of them. No one could forget that they had been burning more fuel because of the hole in the Plexiglas nose, and the sun over Nagoya had been left behind and the weather was rapidly deteriorating.

Two Japanese zero fighter planes gave chase, pulling up behind the B-25, but Will climbed into a bank of gathering clouds and soon lost them. They soon resumed their low altitude, skimming along above the sea. But the glistening, calm water below them soon turned into a raging gray mass as they headed along the southeastern coast of Japan, before striking out over the East China Sea for China. Along the way, they lost sight of planes #14 and #15. They were now on their own.

It was foggy, and darkness was descending when they reached the Chinese coast. George worked feverishly to locate their position on the maps in front of him. North China and most of the Chinese coastal area were under Japanese control, and they wanted to be sure they landed their plane in friendly, free China.

An hour later George announced that they were over Choo Chow Lishui, one of the Doolittle Raiders' rendezvous sites. Will circled the area, calling repeatedly on the radio for anyone below. But he got no answer. The fog cleared a little, and Jake could make out a small town below them, but he could see no airfield. They had no choice but to fly on, hoping for a break in the weather and a landing strip somewhere farther inland.

An hour later, the low-fuel light flashed on in the B-25. Jake busied himself staring below, hoping to see some sign of friendly territory. Will circled above a town at an altitude of three thousand feet looking for a runway, but there wasn't one.

"It's got to be Nanchang," George told Jake over the intercom. "Will says get ready to jump."

Jake remembered that in a briefing back on the USS *Hornet* they had been warned that the Japanese most likely controlled the area around Nanchang. But with no fuel left in the plane's tanks, after thirteen hours aloft, they had no choice but to leave the B-25 bomber behind. They would know soon enough whether the Japanese or the friendly Chinese held the area below.

George was the first to bail out. Jake watched as he dropped out the forward hatch into the darkness. Then it was Jake's turn to jump. He slid his pistol, knife, and ration packets into the pockets of his leather jacket. As he edged toward the open hatch,

he tried to recall all he had been taught during Army
Air Corps training about making a parachute jump.
At that time the closest he had come to making a real
parachute jump was lowering himself with his parachute through the hatch of a bomber parked on the
ground and dropping to the tarmac. But this time he
was three thousand feet above China, and his survival depended on his following the steps he had
been taught in training. He checked the tension on
the harness of his parachute, made sure the handle
of the ripcord was free, and then slowly began lowering himself out the hatch. But no sooner had Jake
dropped his legs through the hatch than the wind
caught them and pressed them back against the
fuselage of the plane. In fact, the wind pressed them
against the plane so hard that Jake had to push with
all his might on the door frame to get out of the hatch.
Then suddenly he felt himself slip free. He began falling into the darkness.

Above him Jake could see the B-25, and when it
had passed over him, he pulled on the ripcord of his
parachute. Moments later he felt an upward jerk. He
knew his parachute had properly opened. He could
hear the drone of the bomber's engines trail away
above him. Jake was now totally on his own, falling
through the darkness over a country in which he had
never before set foot. He felt utterly alone.

Jake was enveloped not only in darkness as he
descended toward the ground but also in dense fog
and rain. He could see nothing and had no way of
telling how close he was to he ground. Then suddenly

his body crashed into the earth with a jolt, and Jake was aware that he was sprawled out and facedown.

After many hours in the air, Jake was back on land. But it wasn't dry land. Rain was pouring down, and he could feel mud squelching through his fingers. Jake rolled over and got to his knees. It was pitch black as he fumbled around and unlatched his parachute. Then, as his eyes adjusted to the darkness, he realized he was kneeling on top of a mound, and there were other mounds of about the same size all around him. Then it dawned on him—he had landed on top of a grave. He chuckled to himself. Of all places to land, he had dropped down right on top of the final resting place of a Chinese man.

Farther out, beyond the mounds, he could see pools of blackness that rippled in the wind. Remembering back to their briefings on the *Hornet*, Jake concluded that these must be flooded rice paddies.

Aware that his four crewmates must have all jumped by now, Jake slid his pistol out of his pocket and shot it into the air. He listened for a response— either a shout or a gunshot—but he could hear only eerie silence.

Suddenly loneliness again overcame him. Had everyone else survived the jump? Would they strike out in the same direction and meet up? If the Japanese occupied the territory, how long would it be before Japanese soldiers found him? Or by some miracle had they bailed out over a Chinese stronghold?

Jake scrambled wearily to his feet. As he stood up, he flinched. Stabbing pain shot through his chest and arms. He steadied himself and took a deep breath—more pain. He took shallow breaths as he unzipped his jacket and felt inside. The pain became unbearable as he felt his rib cage. It was obvious to him that he had broken several ribs when he collided with the ground. He carefully zipped up his jacket and pulled the parachute toward him. He then pulled the knife from his jacket pocket and cut off a length of the parachute fabric. This would give him a little protection from the rain.

With the silk fabric draped over his head and body, Jake stood up and began walking. It didn't much matter in which direction he went; he was surrounded by rice paddies. He sloshed through the mud, bending slightly as he went to lessen the pain of his ribs.

Jake was thoroughly soaked by the time he came to a tiny building, about the size of a broom cupboard. Inside he found some incense holders and concluded that it was probably some kind of shrine. He cleared out the holders and backed inside. The building was just wide enough for him to get in and sit down with his legs pulled up to his chest. The building was not comfortable, but it was dry.

Within minutes of sitting down, Jake was sound asleep. He did not wake up until the sun was up the following morning. When he awoke, it took him several seconds to remember what had happened to him the night before and where he was.

Somewhere in the dark, stormy night Jake had lost his rations, and he had nothing to answer the growl in his stomach. Gingerly, he pressed his hands against either side of the shrine and pulled himself to his feet. He stepped outside, getting his first glimpse of China in the daylight.

The countryside was lush and green, and Jake could see a track leading off to the left. He waded through a rice paddy toward it. He stepped up to the track and started walking. The mud dried and caked to his body and uniform as he walked along. His heart thumped as he saw two men coming in the opposite direction. One was carrying a bucket. As they got closer, Jake waved. Soon they were just feet apart, and Jake started talking slowly. He pointed to the US insignia on his jacket and tried to communicate that he was American. The men looked at each other, said nothing, and moved on. Jake found the men's behavior odd, but it happened again, and then again. No one seemed the least bit interested in a strange white man, filthy from head to toe, walking through rice paddies.

Jake came to a small stall where an old man sat selling colored eggs and vegetables. He felt sure that he would make progress now. He gestured for a pencil and paper and drew a picture of a Chinese insignia and a Japanese insignia on a page and then drew a question mark. The old man shrugged and went back to picking bugs off a cabbage.

Jake could see the old man was not going to be any help either. He walked on, wondering whether people wouldn't talk to him because they were afraid of being punished by the Japanese or because this was Chinese-held territory and no one was interested in the war. He walked past small Chinese houses and was surprised to see that not only people but also chickens and pigs all lived together inside the ramshackle homes.

The farther Jake walked, the more invisible he felt. No one smiled at him or nodded in recognition. It was as if Jake were a ghost to them—albeit a very muddy and hungry ghost. He passed a cluster of houses with several soldiers standing around. Two of them were washing clothes in a ditch. Jake hesitated for a moment. Should he approach them or not? He remembered the advice about telling a Japanese person from a Chinese person by how spread out their toes were. But in military boots, he thought glumly, all toes are equal! Because he didn't want to risk approaching the soldiers, he walked right past the houses. No one shouted at him or tried to intervene.

As Jake continued walking, he realized that he would have to make some kind of move toward someone, as no one was going to initiate any move toward him. His heart began to thump wildly as he saw another house in the distance. This, he decided, was the one he was going to approach for help. He felt for the pistol in his pocket, checked the ammunition clip, and made sure that a bullet was in the firing chamber.

Within minutes Jake was standing at the open doorway of the house. Chickens squawked around his feet. Jake took a deep breath and stepped inside. Sitting at a table were two soldiers playing a game with several local children. Words came out of Jake in a rush, along with a jumbled attempt at sign language. He pointed to himself and said, "American," and mimicked a plane flying overhead. Then he pointed to the older of the two soldiers. "China or Japan?" he asked.

"China," the soldier replied.

But instead of relief at the answer, Jake felt a sense of dread, something was not right. His right hand curled around the trigger of his pistol—he had seven bullets left.

Jake backed up toward the door, when suddenly he was aware of a commotion outside. He turned his head to see ten soldiers, armed with bayonets, pistols, and swords, gathered in the yard. "China or Japan?" he yelled, aware of the desperation in his voice.

"China," one of them yelled back.

Jake smiled and gestured for them to come in. There was nothing else he could do unless he knew for sure they were Japanese, and then there were more of them than bullets in his pistol.

The soldiers slapped Jake on the back and smiled at him. Through the language barrier Jake could tell they were trying to joke with him and make him feel at ease, but he could feel the sweat beading on his forehead.

After a few minutes the soldiers gestured for Jake to come with them, and they left the house together and set out down the road. After about five minutes they stopped for a moment, and Jake turned to find a bayonet pointed against his back. Then, as if on cue, all of the soldiers pointed their weapons at him, and one of them reached into Jake's jacket pocket and pulled out his .45 pistol. Then they walked on as if nothing had happened.

Jake still wasn't sure whether he was in the hands of friends or foes. He could imagine the Chinese not wanting to escort someone who was armed and did not understand a word they said. He could also imagine the Japanese tricking him into walking with them. Which scenario was the right one? He wished he knew.

Eventually the group reached a camp, where a friendly officer greeted them—a good sign, Jake concluded.

Another officer came outside. "Please to be inside with us," he said in fractured English.

Jake smiled weakly and entered the house, knowing that the next few minutes could determine whether he lived or died.

Chapter 7

Captured

The room into which Jake was led was lined with photos of Asian military men, all with numerous ribbons and medals pinned to their chests. Jake studied the photos and asked the interpreter the men's names. He did this to buy himself a little time while he adjusted to his new surroundings, and also in the hope that he might recognize one of the names as either Japanese or Chinese. Unfortunately, this did not happen, and when Jake finally sat down, he still did not know whose hands he was in.

The questions started immediately: "Did you come from an airplane? Where is the plane now? Where are the other airmen who were on board? What are you doing in China? Were you part of the bombing of Japan? If so, where did the planes take off from, and how many planes were there?"

Jake struggled to stay calm as he gave the same answer to almost every question, either "I don't know" or "I won't tell you."

The interrogator smiled. "How about something to eat?" he asked. "You must be very hungry by now."

Jake nodded. "Some food wouldn't be a bad idea," he replied, hoping that he did not sound too hungry and give the idea that he could be made to give answers in exchange for food.

Moments later a peasant woman appeared at the door with a tray of cakes and tea. Jake was offered one of the cakes. It tasted delicious, not quite like anything he'd ever had before, almost like apple butter, but not quite.

The cake eaten, as Jake sipped the tea, the interrogation began again: the same questions, and the same answers. Eventually, the interrogator became impatient and gave a new set of instructions to the interpreter.

"They say to tell you they are Japanese. Do you understand you are in the hands of the Japanese?" the interpreter relayed.

Jake's heart sank. He understood perfectly well.

"Aren't you afraid?" the interpreter asked.

"What should I be afraid of?" Jake replied as a thousand answers to that question raced through his head.

The questioning continued, but Jake continued to stonewall until eventually the interrogator gave some kind of instructions.

Immediately Jake was hauled to his feet and marched out the door. He was escorted at bayonet point down the road for several miles to another compound that looked very similar to the one he had just left. This time he was shut in a room with guards at the door and window. As the time passed, it grew dark and cold, and Jake huddled in the corner for warmth. This was his second night in China. Last night he had hoped that by some miracle he had parachuted into free China. Now, twenty-four hours later, he knew better. He was now a prisoner of war, held by the Japanese.

As the night dragged on, Jake tried not to think about the stories he had heard of how the Japanese treated their prisoners. He remembered hearing that in Japanese culture it was a great shame to be taken alive in battle and that it was honorable to take your own life if you were captured rather than submit to the enemy. That is why, rumor had it, the Japanese were so cruel to their prisoners. They looked down on them as too weak and too cowardly to commit suicide rather than be captured.

Several commotions took place outside his window in the night, and Jake thought he heard American voices. Had some of the other men from the *Bat* been picked up as well?

In the morning Jake was brought into a large room where two other crew members were sitting—Will Farrow and Harold Spatz. Jake nodded in their direction. He longed to talk to them but did not want the Japanese to know they were from the same plane.

Will and Harold were hauled to their feet and marched outside with Jake. In the morning light they had their photographs taken, and then they were marched back inside. Jake wondered what had happened to their other two crewmen. Had they made safe landings? Were they still wandering around the countryside waiting to be captured?

Before long his questions were answered when George Barr and Bob Hite were brought to the compound. Now all five crewmen were in one place. George looked the worst. He was limping from having sprained his ankle and bruised his knee when he landed.

With the arrival of the other two men, the interrogation started up again and went on for much of the day until it finished abruptly. All five men were then blindfolded, handcuffed, and leg cuffed with a chain between so they could walk. A wave of helplessness surged over Jake. As long as he could see his comrades, he had hope. But now all he could see was darkness, and morbid thoughts overcame him: Would the Japanese blindfold them when they killed them? Would they be shot or beheaded?

Time dragged on, and then Jake felt himself being led out of the house and loaded onto a truck. He heard George and Will say a few words and figured that all five of the men were being taken away together.

After a long drive, the five crewmen, still blindfolded and cuffed, were pulled off the truck and led up a ramp. Jake took a deep breath. He knew that smell anywhere—aviation fuel. They were boarding an airplane!

The plane was obviously a military aircraft, and Jake sat on a hard bench with his back against the side of the plane. Inside, the noise from the droning engines was deafening, and the plane seemed to rattle so much that Jake thought it might fall apart in midair. As they flew along, Jake could almost hear his empty stomach screaming out for food.

Blindfolded, Jake lost all sense of how long the flight actually was. Eventually the flight ended, and the men were led off the plane and onto another truck. Soon the truck rumbled to a stop and the men's blindfolds were taken off.

The first thing Jake and his crewmates did was look around and make sure that the other four men were still there. They were, and they marched together to a cell block. It was more primitive than any prison Jake had ever seen before, but it was a prison just the same. The cells were square cages with wooden bars and a dirt floor. The only thing inside each cell was a box, obviously a toilet, since its foul-smelling contents oozed over the top. Jake wanted to gag at the sight and the smell.

Each man was shoved into his own cell, but it was possible to see the other prisoners and the endless parade of guards who patrolled the cell block. Jake wished he knew more about Asia and, in particular, the difference between Japan and China. He couldn't even tell which country he was now in.

That night, Jake and the others were blind-folded once again and taken away one at a time for questioning.

Jake's spirits reached an all-time low when his interrogator pulled out a piece of paper on which was written the names of the Doolittle Raiders—all eighty of them. Being a prisoner of war, Jake had told his captors only his name, rank, and serial number, and he assumed his crewmates had done the same. But along with their names and the paper, the Japanese had enough information to confirm that they had captured the entire crew of the *Bat*.

A new interrogator who spoke flawless English was present and wanted to know exactly what had happened. Jake couldn't see him because his blind-fold had been put back on, but he could smell cigar smoke. "You had better talk," the man said, "because these men are very cruel, and they will torture you until you do speak. Better sooner than later, don't you think?"

Jake held his silence, trying to divert himself from thinking of the various torture techniques that he had heard the Japanese used.

Someone in the room sighed, and Jake was stood up and led into another room, where his blind-fold was removed. A short, squat man with a cigar between his teeth stood in front of him. He took the cigar from his mouth, tapped it deliberately on the desk, nodded at Jake, and then spoke in Japanese. The man who had led Jake into the room interpreted. "I am the kindest judge in all of China. You are very lucky to be standing before me. I want to help you. You tell me the truth, and I get you a glass of milk. You must be hungry and thirsty by now. Right?"

That would have been an easy question for Jake to answer! His stomach was so empty that it felt like it was glued to his backbone. "I won't talk," Jake replied.

The judge continued. "How do you pronounce h-o-r-n-e-t?"

"Hornet," Jake said.

"You know that name, don't you? Your plane was on the aircraft carrier *Hornet*, wasn't it?"

Jake remained silent, worried that the judge's tone of voice had gone from gentle and reassuring to menacing in less than a minute. Clearly these were no friends of his in the room.

"And Colonel Doolittle was your commanding officer, wasn't he?" the judge went on.

"I won't talk," Jake repeated.

"We'll see about that!" the judge sneered as he pulled a long sword from the scabbard on his belt and held it at chest height. The weapon glistened in the pool of light from the overhead electric bulb. "Tomorrow morning, when the sun comes up, I am going to have the honor of cutting off your head."

Jake tried to remain calm—what could he say? He was not going to betray the mission by talking. He decided to turn the threat into a joke, since he didn't appear to have anything to lose. "It would be an honor to have the kindest judge in all of China cut off my head," he replied.

The judge and the other men in the room laughed, and the interrogation session was over for the night.

Jake was once again blindfolded and taken back to his cell. But before he was handcuffed again, a guard brought him a glass of milk. The milk was warm, and it reminded Jake of the fresh milk he drank right from the milking bucket as a boy back in Oregon. He wondered what his family was doing right at that moment. They might have heard of the Doolittle Raid, but they would have no idea that Jake had been a part of it. In time, Jake knew, they would be told some of the facts.

It was a long night, and Jake was kept company by hundreds of lice that invaded his cell and crawled all through his clothes and over his skin. Even if he were not handcuffed, he would have found it impossible to ward them all off.

Jake tried to imagine this being his last night on earth. He thought about how it would feel to get his head chopped off. Probably, he concluded, he wouldn't feel a thing. He thought back to his childhood religion, how his father, Jacob DeShazer, had been a Church of God lay preacher and how his family had always prayed and talked about spending eternity with Jesus. It had been a long time since Jake had thought of such things, and now he couldn't squeeze any kind of meaning out of his parents' religion. He knew that if his mother were there with him, she would tell him to "get right with God, repent of your sins, and ask Jesus to forgive you." The reality of doing that seemed as far away as the stars above him. Jake concluded that whatever happened, he had no control over it, and he was not now going to turn tail and pretend to believe in God.

Eventually the sun arose, and Jake felt its warmth on his skin. Then he heard a guard open the door to his cell. He felt hands behind his head and his blindfold being taken off. Jake was led out of the cell and around to the front of the building. He wondered whether this was where the chopping block was.

Instead of encountering the "kindest judge in all of China" and his sword, however, Jake was confronted with a soldier wielding a camera. The soldier snapped a couple of photos of Jake, and then Jake was loaded into another truck. He was blindfolded and handcuffed once again, and ropes were tied around his chest. Jake assumed that this was so he wouldn't attempt an escape, though the handcuffs and blindfold made this highly unlikely.

Throughout the next twelve hours, Jake was jostled on and off airplanes and trucks. He was fairly sure that some or all of the rest of the crew were with him, because every once in a while he could hear Will or George talking to someone. Because of the gnawing hunger in his stomach, it was becoming more difficult for Jake to concentrate on what was going on around him.

After he had been traveling for what seemed like an eternity, Jake managed to lean against the bulkhead of the airplane they were flying in and rub his head just enough to move his blindfold an inch. Jake tilted back his head slowly so as not to draw attention to himself. He looked down his nose and out the window of the aircraft, where he caught a glimpse of a perfectly conical mountain beneath them. The mountain had a dusting of snow on it. Chills ran up and down Jake's spine as he realized instantly that they were flying over Mt. Fuji, which guarded the western approach to Tokyo. He was being taken to the place that the Doolittle Raiders had bombed.

Jake took a deep breath, hoping to shake off the dread that was settling in the pit of his empty stomach.

Chapter 8

Tokyo

Three hours after spotting Mt. Fuji through the corner of his blindfold on the airplane, Jake was sitting alone in a cell in Tokyo. His hands were still cuffed, and his feet were drawn up to his chest. He shook uncontrollably. He could have blamed this on the cold seeping in under the door, but he knew it was from shock and fear. He and his crewmates were now in the hands of the Kempei-Tai, Japan's dreaded military police. Most military men would rather have found themselves in the hands of the German Gestapo than the Japanese Kempei-Tai.

Jake sighed. He wasn't sure that he or any of the other crew members had information that was particularly valuable to their captors. At their last interrogation stop, the interrogator had brought up the name of the USS *Hornet*, so Jake concluded that the Japanese probably had the idea that they had been transported to some location closer to Japan aboard the *Hornet*. What Jake didn't think they realized was that the bombers had actually taken off from the aircraft carrier, and that was a piece of information they would prize. Jake hoped that he would not divulge the information during the interrogation and torture that he knew was bound to follow soon.

Sure enough, not long after arriving at the prison in Tokyo, Jake was dragged from his cell for his first session of interrogation. He soon learned that these sessions would become torturous. He was led into a room with a table in the middle, behind which sat a Kempei-Tai officer, with an official recorder sitting to the side and three military policemen standing to the side by the wall.

"Well, well," the interrogator began in English after Jake had been brought into the room. Then he began a barrage of questions about the mission of the Doolittle Raiders: From where had they taken off? How many planes participated in the raid? Where did they train? Who was their leader? Where were the planes supposed to refuel in China? The questions went on and on.

From the list of members of the Doolittle Raiders he had been shown in China, Jake surmised that the Japanese already knew the answers to many of the questions they were asking him. He was determined not to answer any of their questions. Instead, to each question he was asked he simply gave his name, rank, and serial number, the only pieces of information a prisoner of war was obliged to give to his captors.

Such answers to the questions did not please Jake's interrogator, however. Before Jake knew it, the military policemen had forced him to his knees and were beating and kicking him. Jake winced with each thud of pain that pulsed through his body. But the truth was, Jake didn't know that much. He was a lowly corporal, not an officer, and had not been privy to the strategic planning of the mission. He simply followed the orders he was given.

After Jake had been beaten he was returned to his cell, bruised and barely conscious. Day after day the routine repeated itself for Jake. Always the interrogator would start with the same words, "Well, well," until in Jake's mind the man's name became *Well, well*. Sometimes, though, Well, well would vary the questions. Instead of wanting to know the specifics of the Doolittle Raid, he wanted to know about America. Where had Jake traveled in America? What did Americans think of the Japanese? Were they afraid of them? Did they expect them to take over the White House? As usual, Jake would remain defiant in the face of the questioning, which in turn led to a beating and his being delivered back to his cell.

In one interrogation session Jake was told that there was a difference of opinion between military headquarters and the War Department as to how the prisoners should be treated. At the War Department, General Sugiyama wanted the men put to death as war criminals, while General Tojo, Japan's premier, saw them as prisoners of war and thought that they should get life in prison for their crimes. So whether or not the crew of the *Bat* lived or died depended on whose opinion eventually prevailed. At that moment Jake didn't much care. Death seemed like a welcome escape from daily beatings.

The interrogations dragged on for eighteen days— eighteen days of beatings, torture, and subsisting on a diet of weak tea and bread. By the end of the eighteen days, Jake could feel every one of his ribs. To make matters worse, he hadn't bathed since he had landed in the graveyard back in China, nor had he spoken to his four crewmates from the *Bat*.

Jake was pretty sure that other Americans were also in the prison. He had heard voices drifting out from other interrogation rooms, and he wondered whether they might be other Doolittle Raiders.

After the eighteen days the Kempei-Tai changed their strategy. They apparently decided to make life a little more bearable for the Doolittle Raiders. Jake was taken from his cell and led into a room where the other four crewmen were also brought. It was hard to look at them. They had changed so much in the three weeks they had been in prison. They were all bloodied and bruised, but Will, who was lanky to begin with, looked like a walking skeleton, and George seemed to bear the marks of the most savage beatings.

Worst of all was the airmen's combined smell. Jake had not had access to water to wash or clean his teeth since being captured by the Japanese, and from the smell of the others, he concluded that they had received the same treatment. The men's clothes were stained and filthy.

The men looked at each other in silence. Jake was sure they were thinking the same thing he was. In the course of their interrogations, had they just unwittingly signed their death warrants and were they about to be executed? Jake didn't know, and a part of him was too tired to even care.

Execution was not in the plans, however. Instead, the men were herded away from their prison block toward the southeast end of the prison. They soon found themselves in an empty block, or at least Jake thought it was empty until one of the guards opened a cell door. Sitting dejectedly inside the cell was a man in a filthy Army Air Corps uniform. Jake peered more closely. It was Lieutenant Chase Nielson, the navigator from plane #6, the *Green Hornet*. The man was emaciated like the rest of them, and from the bruises, blood, and filthy uniform, Jake knew that he had also been tortured by their captors.

While Jake was surprised to see another member of Doolittle's Raiders, he was too tired and sore to care much. Will was pushed into the cell with Lieutenant Nielson, and Jake and Harold were herded into the next cell. Once the lock of the cell door clicked shut, Jake sank to the floor, exhausted from the walk.

Before being captured by the Japanese, Jake imagined that he would have been glad to be reunited with other Doolittle Raiders. But after three weeks of captivity, his mind was foggy, and he wondered whether Harold might have sold out as a Japanese spy. Jake and Harold barely spoke, and from what Jake could hear from the other cells, none of the others were baring their souls to each other either. Besides, the guards beat anyone who did dare to speak. But through a chain of whispers in the night, Jake did learn that Dean Hallmark and Bob Meder, two other members from the *Green Hornet* crew, were also in the cell block, and that the other two crew members, Bill Dieter and Don Fitzmaurice, were dead.

Days passed in the cell block, and the only relief from the boredom was their three "meals" a day. Each meal consisted of a cup of weak tea and two slices of bread, nowhere near enough food to stave off Jake's gnawing hunger. *If they don't execute us soon, we'll starve to death,* Jake thought as he fought back the nauseating weakness from lack of food.

On June 15, 1942, fifty days after the prisoners had been brought to Tokyo from China, there was a change in routine. Jake was once again taken into the interrogation room. This time a guard motioned for him to sit down on a chair by the desk. A piece of paper lay on the desk.

"Well, well. We are asking you to sign this paper now," Jake's interrogator began. "It contains only personal information which we need for our files. If you do not sign it, you will be executed immediately."

The interrogator thrust a pen into his hand, and Jake sighed deeply. What could he do? He looked at the Japanese characters in rows on the paper. They meant nothing to him. For all he knew, he was about to sign a paper begging the emperor of Japan to execute him since he now realized his folly in bombing the land of the rising sun. But what choice did he have? If he did not sign the paper, he was a dead man anyway.

Jake wrote his full name, Jacob Daniel DeShazer. It was the first time he'd held a pen and written his name since signing the crew manifest on the USS *Hornet* over seven weeks ago.

After signing his name, Jake was taken back to his cell, and the next Doolittle Raider was taken away to the interrogation room. Before lunch all eight men had signed papers that they could not read.

Once the papers were signed, events moved swiftly. All eight American airmen were led into the central courtyard. Jake scanned the other seven men, who were all as dirty and unkempt as he was. None of them had bathed or shaved since leaving the *Hornet*. Their hair was matted, and their khaki uniforms were now a dull gray. Dean Hallmark, the *Green Hornet*'s pilot, was limping badly.

As the eight American airmen stood together, lights flashed and they were all photographed, after which they were hurried two at a time into cars and driven away. Soon they pulled up at a train station and were loaded into a waiting train carriage. Because of their combined smell, other passengers in the carriage moved as far away from the men as they could get.

The temperature inside the carriage soon began to rise as more people crowded onto the train. To make matters worse, the train's coal-fired engines billowed an extraordinary amount of soot, which drifted in through the open windows of the carriage, coating everyone with a layer of black grime, though it was hard to notice it on the captured airmen.

The only positive thing about the train trip was that Jake and his fellow captives were fed the same food as the rest of the passengers aboard. For the first time since eating the cake that tasted like apple butter after his capture back in China, Jake was eating something tasty. He wasn't exactly sure what it was that was served with the rice, but the food had flavor, and it wasn't bread. Jake hungrily gulped down everything that he was served. Unfortunately, the rich and tasty food upset his stomach.

As the late afternoon sun, which was beginning to set in the west, filtered in through the carriage windows, Jake was able to work out from the angle of the train to the sun that they were headed in a southwesterly direction. Forty-eight hours later the train pulled into the Nagasaki station, where a military escort was waiting for them. As jarring as the trip had been, Jake was grateful for the six good meals he had been served onboard. He felt stronger already. That night the eight airmen found themselves together in a large, steel cell. No one seemed to care whether they talked together, and no one appeared to be listening.

With food in their stomachs and a change of environment, the men began to talk about their capture. Before long the stories of the crewmen in the *Green Hornet* tumbled out. Unlike the *Bat*, the *Green Hornet* had not quite made it to the Chinese coast. It had run out of fuel four minutes from making landfall in China and only one hundred feet above the sea. The men had had no way to bail out of the B-25, and Dean had tried to belly-land the plane into the ocean. However, the sea was so rough that the waves had thrown the *Green Hornet* back into the air, where it flipped over and landed nose first in the sea. In the process, one of the wings ripped off, and the cabin split open and began to fill with water.

Miraculously, all five crew members had survived the impact and had managed to drag themselves onto the wing of the plane. Several of them, however, had sustained serious injuries. Dean had large gashes in both his legs; gunner/engineer Don Fitzmaurice had a deep hole bashed into his forehead; and bombardier Bill Dieter, in the nose of the plane, had banged his head sharply on impact. Navigator Chase Nielsen had suffered only a broken nose, and copilot Bob Meder had escaped pretty much unscathed.

As Bob tried to inflate the rubber life raft, the cord that operated the CO_2 canister broke. The life raft was useless. Before they could come up with an alternative plan to get to shore, a wave washed the men off the wing into the icy sea. Bob could see that Don was not going to make it to shore on his own, so he grabbed his life jacket and began towing the gunner ashore.

It had taken Bob four hours to make it to shore, and when he did, he found Don unconscious. Bob had tried to revive Don with the mouth-to-mouth resuscitation techniques they had been taught on the *Hornet,* but it was to no avail. Don had died. A short distance away, Bob had found the body of bombardier Bill Dieter. Dean and Chase had been washed ashore farther along the beach and managed to crawl to safety.

At dawn each of the three surviving airmen had been captured by a group of Chinese guerillas, and the three of them were reunited in a local village. The following day the three airmen watched as their two crewmates were buried by the guerillas. They said a prayer for Bill and Don. They told the crew of the *Bat* that they thought about what Jimmy Doolittle had said before they all left on the mission: "Some will come home as heroes. Others as angels."

The next morning Captain Ling, leader of the Chinese guerillas, had arranged for the three survivors to be taken downriver in a sampan to the city of Wenchow. The men were taken to a safe house, but unfortunately Ling had betrayed them. Before long, Captain Ling had led Japanese soldiers to the house, where they had arrested Don, Chase, and Bob.

From there the three survivors' story was a lot like that of the crew of the *Bat.* The men had been interrogated in China by the Japanese and brought to Tokyo for further interrogation and torture.

The five members of the *Bat* crew then told their stories of bailing out over Nanchang, China, and how each of them had eventually been arrested.

By the time night fell, Jake and the others were all exhausted. The two crews now knew each other's story, but what about the crews of the other fourteen bombers? Were they scattered around Japan and China, being interrogated and beaten as well? This was a depressing thought.

The following morning all eight men were led in handcuffs and shackles down to the waterfront and marched onto a ship. As far as Jake could figure out, their only possible destination was China—again.

Chapter 9

Bridge House

For whatever reason, the Japanese sent the Doolittle Raiders they had captured from Japan back to China. When the ship that carried the American airmen from Nagasaki docked in Shanghai on June 19, 1942, Jake felt deflated. He was sure the others also felt the same way. Throughout the voyage he had been hoping that an American submarine would torpedo the ship, giving them some chance of escape, or at least a quick death. But it had not happened.

As Jake shuffled his shackled feet down the gangplank and off the ship, he looked around. Ships and small Chinese junks were everywhere, including the wrecks of several British freighters that had obviously been sunk during the Japanese assault on, and capture of, Shanghai. Dean Hallmark, pilot of the *Green*

Hornet, was too weak from his leg wounds to walk, and was carried from the ship on a stretcher.

On the dock the men were shoved into the back of a truck and driven a short distance to a modern-looking building. "Welcome to Bridge House," one of the guards sneered as the prisoners were led inside.

Jake's pulse raced. He had heard the name "Bridge House" somewhere before, perhaps on the USS *Hornet.* He wasn't exactly sure where he had heard of it, but he knew that before the war the Bridge House in Shanghai had been an English hotel, which the Japanese had converted into a prison for the political prisoners they held in China. It was supposedly one of the most notorious and horrific prisons in Asia.

It did not take Jake and the others long to find out exactly how bad the prison was. The men were thrown into a holding cell on the bottom floor. The cell was more like a bamboo cage, set twenty-four inches off the ground. Jake estimated it to be about twenty feet long by six feet wide, about the size of a boxcar. Inside were thirty of the most wretched people Jake had ever seen. Even his nightmares could not conjure up a more hopeless vision of desperation.

Most people barely looked up as the eight airmen were pushed into the cell and the door locked behind them. Everyone was seated cross-legged, staring at the cell door, and some of the men had to move to make way for Dean and his stretcher. The rest of the airmen, including Jake, followed the lead of the other prisoners and sat down, though they had barely enough room to do so. As Jake sat down, a man nearby groaned and rolled over. A guard rushed up to the side of the bamboo cell and poked him with a stick. The man righted himself and continued his pointless vigil of staring at the door.

As the time ticked away, a guard came back and yelled something at those in the cell. Jake began to wonder how long the guards would leave everyone together like this in the cell. But as he looked around, another thought struck him. Maybe this wasn't a holding cell at all. Maybe this was his new home and these people were all his permanent cellmates.

Hours seemed to pass before food was brought to them. Jake gagged when he looked into the chipped enamel bowl that was slid in through an opening in the cell door. Inside was a scoop of rice and some gray liquid with fatty blobs floating on top. Writhing around inside the bowl were several maggots and worms. As hungry as he was, Jake took one look at the bowl and handed it to the person beside him. There was no way he could swallow the food it contained.

It was summer in China, and the heat inside the cell was stifling. When the guards brought thin blankets and handed one to each of the eight airmen, Jake guessed that it was nighttime. Those in the cell were then allowed to move around a little and find somewhere to sleep. But there was not enough room for everyone to lie down. About half the prisoners were able to recline, while the rest slept sitting up, leaning on each other for support. Jake felt like he was an animal herded into a pen. Despite the fact that it was night, the lights continued to blaze overhead, casting strange shadows over the group. Jake could hear quiet groans and weeping as the night dragged on.

About midnight, another sound drifted into the cell. At first Jake thought he was dreaming, but the sound was real. An orchestra started up, and then a voice began to sing:

> *They asked me how I knew*
> *My true love was true.*
> *Oh, I of course replied*
> *Something here inside cannot be denied.*

> *They said someday you'll find*
> *All who love are blind.*
> *Oh, when your heart's on fire*
> *You must realize*
> *Smoke gets in your eyes.*

Someone not far away was listening to an American pop record. Jake shut his eyes for a moment. He could picture Fred Astaire whirling Ginger Rogers around the dance floor. And then he opened his eyes again to the mass of suffering around him. The music played on, a cruel reminder of everything he had left behind in the United States. He wondered what his mother was doing right then. Did she know he was alive? Had she been told about the Doolittle Raiders' mission? Either way, Jake knew she would be worried sick. He wished he had some way of communicating with the outside world. The Geneva Convention allowed prisoners of war to send letters home, but the Japanese would have none of it.

As the night wore on, rats ran in and out of the cell, scavenging for grains of rice that had fallen and nibbling at any exposed fingers and toes. Despite the stifling heat, Jake tucked his pants legs into his socks and stuffed his hands into his pockets to make himself a less-appealing snack for the vermin.

The music eventually stopped. In the morning the guards came by and prodded everyone with swords until all the prisoners stood up. Many had to lean against the bamboo bars or on one another for support. Minutes later breakfast was served—the same inedible gruel from the night before—and Jake gave his bowl to the young Chinese man next to him. He bowed and thanked Jake, exposing a few broken teeth as he smiled.

The day was long. There was too much time to think and nothing to think about except the terrible conditions Jake found himself in. Everyone in the cell, except Dean, was made to sit cross-legged on the floor. Jake's back ached, and he longed to be able to lean against the cell wall. The temperature inside the cell continued to rise and, with it, the stench of captives and the overflowing "toilet," the barrel in the corner that the Japanese called a "benjo." When the guards weren't looking, the other prisoners picked lice out of their hair and the seams of their clothing. Jake and the other Doolittle Raiders followed their lead.

As the insects crawled over their clothes and from one person to the next, Jake wondered how many diseases the thirty prisoners in the cell could count among them. It was one thing to make it through the torture and the beatings but quite another to survive the deadly diseases around him.

Eventually dinner was doled out in enamel bowls to the prisoners, and then everyone settled for the night. During the night Jake noticed that the guards came by the cell less frequently.

An older Chinese man died quietly in the corner of the cell during the night, and his body was removed in the morning. If the prisoners in the cell continued to die at one per night, Jake mused, no one would be left alive by the end of a month.

Jake didn't like to think of it, but he was having serious doubts about how long Dean from the *Green Hornet* crew would last. Both of Dean's legs had been deeply gashed when the Mitchell B-25 bomber had ditched in the ocean, and now the wounds were infected. The infection, coupled with the lack of food, had sapped the pilot's strength. The normally two-hundred-pound pilot had lost over sixty pounds since being captured by the Japanese. Dean now barely had the strength to move and would often pass out. Jake could see that Dean was fading fast.

By the third day of being cooped up in the wretched cell, Jake was feeling weak and nauseated from hunger. He knew that he would have to give in and eat the prison food served him. As Jake gulped down the contents of the bowl, the food tasted every bit as wretched as it looked. Jake tried not to look too hard at what he was actually putting into his mouth. He tried to reassure himself with Chase Nielsen's comment from the night before that bugs and maggots in the food might provide some vitamins and nutrients that the prisoners' bodies needed. Worst of all for Jake, however, despite the effort of forcing himself to eat, the food did not fill up his hungry stomach.

The days dragged on, punctuated by violent outbursts from the guards. If a prisoner seemed to be relaxing by leaning back on his or her elbows, a guard would strike them with a stick. On some nights, for no apparent reason, the guards would wake everyone up by poking each person with sticks and then would order the person to stand up for the rest of the night. At times like this, all Jake could think of was those carefree days working for the Basque sheepherders, when he was completely alone, with no one telling him what to do. How far away those days were now.

About every other day the Kempei-Tai took a couple of the Doolittle Raiders into a small room and beat or tortured them. Jake used his hatred of the Japanese and their master plan to take over the world to stay mentally focused during these torture sessions.

Then one afternoon, without any fanfare, all of the prisoners except the eight Doolittle Raiders were ordered out of the cell, handcuffed together in twos, and marched away. A dreadful feeling overcame Jake as he watched them go. Were they being marched off to face a firing squad? Or were they being taken to an even worse prison or to some other unimaginable destination? No one knew.

During the time in the cell in Shanghai, the American airmen noticed that their guards were reluctant to unlock the door and actually come into the cell. They used this knowledge to their advantage. Throughout the day the men were supposed to sit cross-legged on the cell floor in silence. But now that the eight Americans were alone together, they began to talk among themselves. Whenever a guard heard them, he would bang on the cell door and yell, "Kurah!" ("Hey" in Japanese.) This meant that the men were supposed to stop talking. But because they knew of the guards' reluctance to enter the cell, they ignored the warning and kept talking. Sometimes Bob Hite would even yell abuse back at the guards.

During these times of talking, each man told the others where he was from, about his experiences growing up, how he came to be in the Army Air Corps, and what he hoped to do back home once America defeated the Japanese. Despite his grim surroundings, Jake enjoyed these times. It lifted his spirit to hear the others talk about life in the United States.

Sometimes, though, the tension in the cell reached a breaking point. On one occasion a new guard came on duty and caught the men talking among themselves. He banged loudly on the door and yelled, "Kurah!" As he often did, Bob yelled back, "Blow it out your barracks bag, buster!" And then he made a threatening gesture with his fists toward the cell door.

Much to everyone's shock, the cell door flung open, and the guard burst into the cell, holding his sword still encased in its scabbard. He swung the sword at Bob and the scabbard hit Bob on the head, leaving a nasty gash. In reflex, Bob reached up and grabbed the scabbard, which pulled away from the sword. Now the guard stood with his highly polished sword ready to thrust it into Bob. Jake held his breath and watched in horror. He quickly glanced at the other men and knew that they were all thinking the same thing. If the guard stabbed Bob with the sword, the men would all rush the guard and strangle him before any other guards could come to his rescue. As the men waited for the guard to strike, Will stood up beside Bob as if to say to the guard, "If you stab him, you are also going to have to stab me."

Both men crouched down like wrestlers ready to pounce. The guard, sensing he was in danger, slowly began to back out of the cell door, locking it behind him. Relief flooded through the cell. After the incident, the guards seemed to have more respect for their American prisoners, and some unexpected things happened.

One of the guards, who spoke English with a British accent, announced that some English policemen were still living and keeping order in the International Concessions of Shanghai. These policemen had taken up a food collection for any American or English prisoners held in the Bridge House. Jake and the other airmen were astonished when soon afterward they were each presented with a plate of deviled eggs, roast beef, corn, and jam roly-poly (a traditional British pudding), followed by a cup of strong coffee.

It was almost too good to believe. Each man savored the taste of home cooking. Jake felt instantly stronger, and his outlook began to improve. Perhaps the Japanese were "fattening them up" before they released them from prison!

Once a day for the next fourteen days, the men enjoyed the wonderful food. And then the meals stopped coming as abruptly as they had started. No explanation was offered as to why.

When the Japanese arrested the airmen, the men's wallets, loose change, watches, rings, and other jewelry items were taken from them. To their surprise, the airmen had been allowed to keep their American banknotes. As the men talked among themselves, they wondered whether one or other of the guards with their new grudging respect for them might be able to be bribed with the money. It took three weeks to hatch their plan, but eventually they spoke to the English-speaking guard. They asked the guard if he would take their pooled American money and exchange it for them on the black market. They waited anxiously, hoping that the guard wouldn't report their action to his superiors. To their relief he did not, and several days later the guard handed them a roll of local banknotes. His action was a surprise to Jake, who puzzled over the strange code of honor that the Japanese guards seemed to have. The guards would beat and humiliate their prisoners for no apparent reason, but they would not steal the prisoners' money.

With the money, the airmen persuaded the guards to bring them meat and candy. It was hard to tell just what kind of meat it was that the guards brought them, but nonetheless, it tasted good to the men. And while they discovered that the candy bars were moldy when they unwrapped them, the candy still tasted good.

As surprised as Jake and the others were at their guards' changing their money on the black market and providing the items they asked for, they had an even bigger surprise in mid-August. It was now four months since the Japanese had captured them, and in that time the men had not bathed, cleaned their teeth, or shaved. Then one day guards came and escorted the men, one at a time, upstairs to one of the old hotel rooms, where the men were allowed to take a bath.

Jake eagerly awaited his turn to bathe. He could hardly wait to get to the top of the stairs and into the bath. He tore off his uniform and climbed in. The bath-water enveloped him in a wave of pure luxury. What was even better, his body floated almost weightless in the water, bringing him relief from the pressure of the boils that had formed on his body in the past weeks. There was another thing he savored—being alone. The guard waited outside the bathroom, leaving Jake completely on his own for the first time since his capture.

There was no time limit on how long each man could stay in the bath, and Jake lost track of how long he stayed in the tub, floating, relaxing, and using up a whole bar of soap scrubbing his body. Another luxury awaited Jake after he climbed out of the bathtub and dried himself off. His stringy beard was trimmed and his head was shaved, sending his matted hair falling to the floor. Then he was given a new set of clothes to put on, and his old uniform was taken away. As he walked downstairs to join the other men, Jake felt like a new man.

As if bathing weren't enough, that night the prisoners were served a hearty meal of steak and fresh vegetables, with strawberry jam and French bread. Jake gobbled the food down, marveling at just how good strawberry jam tasted smeared on bread.

Yet as he settled down for the night, a question ran through Jake's mind: Why? After four months, why had they suddenly been allowed to bathe and put on new clothes? And why had they been fed such a good meal? Why? Why? Why? Jake wished he knew the answer. Given the way their Japanese captors had treated them over the past four months, their captors surely hadn't had a change of heart about the Americans' treatment. There had to be a reason why the men had been given baths and a good meal.

Chapter 10

Guilty

On August 28, 1942, a week after the eight airmen had taken their first bath in four months, the lock clicked, their cell door swung open, and the men were ordered outside. A stretcher was brought in for Dean, and Will and Bob Hite each took an end of it. Outside the cell, guards handcuffed and shackled each man and then marched them all outside into the daylight. Jake shielded his eyes against the bright glare.

It had been seventy days since Jake and the other airmen had entered the Bridge House Jail, and each man had lost about fifty pounds during his time there. The men's hair was thin, their balance wobbly, and their spirits low. Jake knew that the others were all thinking the same thing he was thinking: where were they being taken?

The men were hauled up onto the back of a truck and driven off through the streets of Shanghai. Jake wondered whether they were headed for the countryside to be executed. As it turned out, they were taken to the Kiangwan Military Prison, several miles away on the outskirts of Shanghai. At Kiangwan the prisoners were unloaded from the truck and escorted into a cell block, where each man was assigned to his own nine-feet-long by five-feet-wide, concrete-walled cell.

The following morning the prisoners were taken from their cells and marched into a large room with a single long table set in the middle. After they entered the room, a guard yelled at the airmen to stand at attention. The airmen did not, however, attempt to lift Dean from his stretcher.

Jake tried to steady himself as three Japanese men, wearing the traditional garb of English barristers, solemnly walked into the room. In another time and place, Jake would have been amused by these short, brown-skinned men wearing long, curly black wigs and long black gowns, but the atmosphere in the room—which Jake now realized had turned into a courtroom—was deadly serious.

To one side of the table stood a translator, who introduced himself as Caesar Luis de Remedios. The half Portuguese, half Japanese man had been convicted of spying for the Allies and was serving a seven-year prison sentence. Because he spoke four languages (among them English) fluently, he had been put to work as an interpreter.

Each Doolittle Raider was asked to step forward and answer a few basic questions about himself: What was his name? What was his rank? Where was he from? Why had he joined the American military?

Jake and the others answered briefly, and de Remedios relayed their answers to the three Japanese judges. The proceedings then continued in Japanese, with no more translation into English. Neither Jake nor any of the others could understand what was being said. By watching carefully, however, Jake concluded that the judges were reading and reviewing a series of documents. At one stage the judges asked each man to verify that it was his signature on the paperwork being reviewed.

Jake's heart sank when he was asked to verify his signature. He knew that the only time he had signed anything since being taken prisoner had been in the jail in Tokyo when he had been tortured and forced to sign something in Japanese. He had been told at the time that all he was signing was a document containing personal information that his captors needed for their files. Now he began to wonder whether he had unwittingly signed a "confession."

The trial lasted for several hours. It was painful for Jake to be standing for that long and even more painful to be watching Dean in his delirious state slip in and out of consciousness. George wasn't faring too well either. He fainted early in the proceedings, and the judges allowed him to sit on a chair.

Eventually the three judges gathered up all of the papers, bowed to each other, and left the room. Caesar

Luis de Remedios turned to the airmen. "They asked me not to tell you what they have decided," he said, as he, too, made a hasty exit.

The words were difficult to hear. Jake felt completely in limbo. Was he about to be executed? Returned to the solitary confinement of his cell? Tortured some more? He had no idea, and at this dark moment, no one option sounded better or worse than the other.

Jake and six of the other Doolittle Raiders were taken back to their cells, while two guards carried Dean on his stretcher down the corridor. As Jake watched Dean disappear, he wondered whether he would ever see the pilot of the *Green Hornet* again.

Life at Kiangwan Military Prison soon fell into its own monotonous routine. The meals were the same horrible rice soup they had been served at the Bridge House Jail, supplemented with sawdust-laden bread. The men were taken out of their cells each morning and allowed to wash their hands, clean their teeth, and exercise for ten minutes. Then it was back into their cell for the remainder of the day. The prisoners were not permitted to communicate with each other, and this worried Jake the most. Jake's thoughts often turned to Dean. Was he getting any kind of medical attention or better food rations?

With the passing of each dreary day Jake became more incensed with the way the Japanese were treating him and his fellow airmen. Every soldier knew about the Geneva Convention, which stipulated how prisoners were to be treated. A prisoner of war was entitled to visits from the Red Cross, mail from home, and communication with the American consulate. But Jake had received none of these.

Twenty days later, on October 15, 1942, Jake was taken from his cell at 9:00 AM and told to wash himself in a basin of water. The weather was foggy and cool. It was not the weather, however, that sent chills down Jake's back. It was the sight of several Chinese prisoners walking past, carrying shovels. His interest piqued, Jake looked around more closely and noticed that several of the guards were wearing their dress uniforms, the kind of uniform that signified some special event was about to take place.

Jake's hands shook as he buttoned up his shirt. Was the "special" occasion their execution? Were the Chinese prisoners going to dig the airmen's graves?

Despite Jake's foreboding, nothing happened to him that day, and the next day he was taken back to the room where the "trial" had taken place. Jake's spirit sagged as he found himself back in the courtroom standing at attention with Bob Hite, George Barr, Bob Meder, and Chase Nielsen. But Jake's spirit sagged even further when he realized that Will, Harry, and Dean were missing. Jake had caught a glimpse of both Will and Harry two days before, but he had not seen Dean in the nearly two months since their trial.

About fifteen Japanese officers were crowded into the makeshift courtroom, and the same judges, wearing their ridiculous wigs, sat behind the long table. Jake wondered whether he and the others were going to be tried all over again.

When everyone was in place, the chief judge nod-ded to de Remedios, who began reading from a sheaf of papers. "It has been proven beyond all doubt that the defendants, motivated by a false sense of glory, carried on indiscriminate bombing of schools and hospitals and machine-gunned innocent civilians with complete disregard for the rules of war…"

Jake took a deep breath as his befuddled brain tried to get a handle on what was being said. They had never fired on schools or hospitals, and the mili-tary targets they had bombed had been meticulously chosen so that innocent civilians would *not* be killed. He even remembered how some of the Raiders had wanted to bomb the emperor's palace in Tokyo, but Jimmy Doolittle had strictly forbidden them to do so. Bitterly, Jake now wished they had bombed the place.

The interpreter continued in his strange accented English. "The tribunal finds the defendants guilty of Sections 1 and 2 of Article 2 of the Military Law con-cerning the Punishment of Enemy Airmen. There-fore, the military tribunal has passed judgment and imposes sentences under the provisions of Article 3 of that law. The tribunal, acting under the law…sen-tences the defendants to death!"

Caesar Luis de Remedios paused. Not a sound was heard in the courtroom. Jake saw Chase strain forward. As Chase did so, a guard raised his rifle and aimed it at Chase's stomach.

With a cough, de Remedios shuffled his pages and read on. "Through the graciousness of His Majesty, the Emperor, your sentences are hereby commuted to life imprisonment with special treatment." The interpreter wiped his brow with a handkerchief. His job done, he stepped behind the protection of the guards. In unison the guards formed a ring around the five airmen.

Jake tried to think what the words he'd just heard meant, but his brain was fuzzy from lack of food. Would the "special treatment" be good treatment or ongoing torture? And where were Dean, Will, and Harry? The men had no opportunity to ask questions, and they were marched back to their cells to continue with solitary confinement.

Over the next two days, as he sat alone in his cell, Jake came to believe that the other three airmen had been executed. It made some sense, as Will and Dean had piloted two of the planes that took part in the raid on Japan, and they were the two senior ranking officers among them. But what about Harry? Jake could not understand why he would have been executed. After all, like Jake, Harold was an enlisted man, the lowest in rank among the captured airmen.

The following day Jake and the other four airmen were told that their "special treatment" included one bath a week, a shave and haircut, and the opportunity to wash out their underwear and shirts. It was more than Jake had hoped for.

Days dragged into weeks as Jake sat alone in his tiny cell. He spent most of his time staring at the wall, though he did begin to compose poetry in his head to help pass some of the time. The only bright spot in this ordeal was de Remedios. Not only was he used as an interpreter in the prison, but also he was a trusty who was allowed out of his cell to assist the guards. One of his jobs was delivering the meager meals to the prisoners. As he slid the bowls of food through the slot in the cell door, he would often slip a balled-up piece of paper into the prisoner's hand. Jake loved to receive these notes from him, and he knew the trusty was taking a risk by secretly passing them along. Sometimes the notes told how the other prisoners were doing in solitary confinement, and sometimes they brought news of what was happening beyond the prison doors. One day he slipped a note into Jake's hand that read, "Japanese newspaper says big naval battle fought off Midway Island. I think they lost. War will soon be over. You will go home soon."

Jake appreciated the news and the encouragement, but as much as he wished he could go home, he doubted that he would ever see the United States again. He was certain, given what he had learned about the Japanese mindset during his imprisonment, that his captors would never release him alive, that he would most likely be executed before American soldiers arrived to liberate him and the other airmen.

As winter descended over Shanghai, the weather became bitter cold. With no heating in the cell block, conditions inside the cells became almost unbearable for Jake and the others. Jake now spent most of his days shivering, wrapping his arms around himself in a vain attempt to keep warm. One day de Remedios had passed a note to Jake saying that he was aware of their plight and was trying to get them warmer clothes and blankets. In this regard, December 5, 1942, was a red-letter day for Jake. That day the door to his cell swung open. Jake was taken from his cell, marched down the corridor and around the corner, and deposited into a large cell. Inside were Bob Hite, George Barr, Bob Meder, and Chase Nielsen. Before he locked the cell door, the guard threw fifteen blankets into the cell. Jake laughed out loud. Three blankets apiece! One to lay on the cold floor beneath him and two to pull over him for warmth. It was almost too good to be true.

For Jake, what was even better than getting three blankets was to again be with the other men. A babble of noise quickly filled the cell as the airmen rushed to say all they wanted to say to the others before they were once again parted and led back to their cells for more solitary confinement. To Jake's surprise, however, no guard came to escort him or any of the other men away. The new cell arrangement appeared to be long-term, and Jake settled into the comfort of the company of his comrades.

Jake had not looked in a mirror since they had taken off from the USS *Hornet* on the morning of the raid, almost eight months before. But now looking at the sight of the other men, he could only imagine how bad he looked. They had all lost weight since being brought to Kiangwan Military Prison. Their belts were cinched up, their skinny bodies were emaciated, and their faces were gaunt and their cheeks sunken. Like the others, Jake could press his thumb into his leg bones and leave a permanent dent. He knew from Doc White's first-aid lectures back on the *Hornet* that this was a sure sign of beriberi, a nerve disease brought on by a lack of vitamin B_1 and prevalent among people whose sole sustenance consisted of white polished rice, even if the portions they ate were small. Jake knew that other symptoms of the disease included lack of concentration and muscle pain.

After several days, once the men ran out of things to talk about, Bob Meder took over the "social activities," as he called them. Bob spent hours devising various games that the men could play to keep their minds active. He held a spelling bee, and there were quizzes to name state capitals, presidents, and the dates of various historical events. Bob also ran a lottery, and the man whose number was drawn would receive an extra half bowl of rice soup from the others. They also would draw lots on the order the bowls were passed through the slot in the cell door at mealtimes. Again the winner would receive an extra half bowl of soup from the others.

One of the favorite games that Bob introduced was the "flea-lice catch game," which the men played every Sunday morning. The men's fifteen blankets were piled up, and one blanket was laid out on the cell floor. The men then sat around the blanket, and when a signal was given, they proceeded to catch as many lice and fleas on the blanket as possible. The game continued until all fifteen blankets had been laid out and gone over.

The lice were white, fairly slow moving, and relatively easy to see and catch on the blanket, and each man received a point for every louse he caught. However, the fleas were dark, fast moving, and much harder to catch, and each man received five points for each flea he caught. The winner was the man with the most points. Jake enjoyed the game. Not only did it get the men laughing and passing the time, but also it fulfilled a practical function—delousing and defleaing their blankets once a week.

Once a week the men rotated where they sat. They took turns receiving the bowls of food as they were slid through the cell door and gathering the enamel bowls and cups and the chopsticks after they had eaten.

Since the men were now all together in one cell, it was easier for them to get information from Caesar Luis de Remedios. They no longer had to worry about finding out how the others were holding up in their cells and were now able to concentrate on gaining information about the world beyond their cell block. De Remedios was a lifeline. He fed the men any scrap of information about the war that he found in the local newspaper. For hours on end, the men would then discuss and dissect the information in every possible way.

One piece of information that kept Jake and the others occupied for hours was the fact that de Remedios had discovered other Americans in the prison. Over a series of days, the trusty managed to convey to the men that the names of the two prisoners were

Commander Cunningham and Corporal Battles, both of whom had been captured when the Japanese over-ran Wake Island.

Jake also was heartened to learn that de Remedios had alerted the two other Americans to the presence of five of the Doolittle Raiders in the same prison with them. Now two more men knew of their survival after the raid and might be able to get word home to their families in the United States.

One day, eight months after arriving at Kiangwan Military Prison, Jake and the other four airmen were handcuffed, blindfolded, roped together, and led out to a waiting truck. Tomorrow, April 18, 1943, marked the anniversary of their bombing raid over Japan. Jake's stomach lurched as he contemplated the next few hours. Was more retaliation coming his way as the Japanese commemorated the attack?

Chapter 11

Everything Was New
and Alive

Jake and the other four Doolittle Raiders sat silently as the truck rumbled along. Little was said throughout the journey as they all contemplated what might be about to happen to them. Jake had held out the vague hope that they would be reunited with Dean, Will, and Harry, but these men were nowhere to be seen. Despite his best efforts, Jake found himself thinking about the three men's probable deaths and hoping that their executions had been swift.

When the truck came to a halt, the men were transferred to an airplane, and a short while later they were airborne. The flight lasted about an hour. When they landed, George and Chase, both trained navigators, whispered that from the landmarks they had been able to spot as they peeked out of the corner of their blindfolds during the flight, they were in Nan-king, northwest of Shanghai.

In Nanking they were taken from the airplane to another prison. This prison, with its shiny metal doors and fresh paint, appeared to be new. But Jake's heart dropped when he realized that he and his friends were once again being put into solitary confinement. Jake braced himself for the endless hours he would have to spend alone again. He pondered a comment that Chase had made one day back at Kiangwan Military Prison. Chase had observed that the hardest thing to do was nothing at all. He said that the human mind and body were made to do things and noted how torturous it became when that was taken away and a man was left with nothing to do.

The only consolation for Jake was that he was put in the smallest cell, he presumed because he was the shortest of the Doolittle Raiders. That the cell measured only five feet by five feet wasn't the good news. The good news, as Jake discovered, was that since the walls were only five feet apart, he was able to climb up them by placing his feet and hands on opposite walls. In this manner he could inch his way up to the tiny vent window about ten feet up the wall. There he was rewarded with a view of the countryside. How wonderful it was to catch a glimpse of people going about their business. Of course, he could climb the walls only when no one was watching. He had no idea what the punishment for such an activity would be, and he did not want to find out.

Jake enjoyed another pleasant surprise at the Nanking prison. Since the place was so new, it was not yet infested with lice, fleas, or rats.

Yet another surprise was in store for Jake at the prison. A short while after his arrival there, a desk and chair were brought into the cell and nailed down to the floor. In Jake's case the desk and chair created a challenge to sleep around, but it was a challenge Jake was willing to endure to have a chair to sit on and a desk to lean against during the day. Jake fantasized about having a book to read or some paper to write on. During the past few months, he'd composed a lot of poetry in his head, but it was difficult to keep all the poems straight in his mind without writing them down.

In other ways, though, the new prison was a disaster. The men's food rations were cut to one small bowl of rice and one bowl of watery soup served twice a day. Also, the men were allowed to exercise together for only fifteen minutes each day.

The five airmen found a way to communicate with each other despite the fact that they were in their own cells in solitary confinement. As part of their Army Air Corps training, each man had learned Morse code. The men worked out a system whereby a tap on the cell wall was a dot, and a scratch was a dash. In this way Jake and the others were able to send and receive messages from the man in the next cell.

As the weeks in the prison slowly dragged on, Jake realized that the prison guards were almost as bored as their prisoners, and some interactions between the two groups started to take place. The guards would brag about how the Japanese were winning every battle they fought, yet from the names of the battles Jake could tell that the Allies were getting closer to the islands of Japan. Of course, this realization didn't make sense. If the Japanese were really winning the war, they surely should be storming the US mainland by now. The fact that they weren't gave Jake hope that someday the Allies would win. When he mentioned this to the guards, they laughed and declared that it did not really matter to the prisoners who won the war. One way or another they would never see their homeland again. If by some great misfortune the Japanese did lose, the guards had orders to behead all "war criminals" before the Allies had a chance to find and liberate the prisoners.

The long, hot summer gave way to fall, and then winter—the coldest winter on record—descended over Nanking. The men were given warmer clothes, which they wore over their existing clothes, but with no body fat, Jake found it impossible to keep warm. He also was concerned about Bob Meder, who showed up for exercise every morning but was unable to do much more than lift his arms into the air.

Over the past several months, all of the men had noticed the deterioration in Bob's condition. Bob was severely ill and looked gaunt and weak. His hip bones stuck out through his pants, and his eyes were sunken and black. Jake guessed that Bob now weighed no more than eighty pounds. Bob looked more and more like a walking skeleton than a human being. By mid-November Bob's condition had deteriorated further, and his legs were swollen from beri-beri. Bob was able to make it out to the exercise yard each day, but once there, he was so weak that all he could do was sit and stare. Despite his condition, Bob never complained to the other men. He simply accepted his condition. It was obvious to Jake and the others that he was near death.

On December 1, 1943, Jake heard several men hammering and sawing in the courtyard. He clambered up the wall and looked through the small window. What he saw chilled his heart. The men were building a coffin. Jake shut his eyes, hoping that his runaway thoughts were wrong. But they were not.

The next day the cell door opened, and Jake was led down the corridor to Bob Meder's cell. Inside was a coffin on top of the desk, and in the coffin lay Bob's body. The guards had laid a wreath of flowers on his chest. As he stared down at Bob's body, Jake wanted to weep, but he fought back the tears, not wanting to give the guards the satisfaction of seeing him cry. Instead, he looked stoically down at his friend. In the twenty months that they had been fellow prisoners, Bob was the one who had excelled at keeping everyone's spirits up, telling the others not to give up, that one day they would all be free. And now Bob Meder was gone. Jake wondered whether any of the rest of them would live long enough to tell what horrors had happened to them since their capture by the Japanese.

Back in his cell, Jake found his thoughts turning to an incident with Bob just a few weeks before. The guards had lightened up a little and allowed the Doolittle Raiders to weed the courtyard. Jake and Bob had ended up working side by side. Looking back on their conversation, Jake realized that Bob probably knew that he was going to die. Bob had wanted to talk about God and why the war was dragging on. "You know," he said to Jake, "I do believe that Jesus Christ is the Lord and Coming King, and that He is God's Son. God expects the nations and people everywhere to recognize Him as Lord and Savior, and the war is not going to stop until Jesus Christ causes it to stop."

The words had seemed to Jake to be out of place. Bob had a brilliant mind yet rarely talked about his faith. As they weeded together that day, however, Bob was telling Jake that he believed God had it all under control.

Pondering Bob's words took Jake back to his childhood, where he had heard his stepfather and mother say similar things a million times. Deep down Jake wished he also could believe those words. Yet Jake could not bring himself to believe. He had too many unanswered questions about faith and God.

Bob's body was removed from the prison the following day. Several days later his ashes were returned to the cell in which he had died and were placed in a small box on the desk. As the ashes were returned to the cell, Jake pondered how anyone, even Jesus, could dare to suggest that a person should love his enemies when his enemies were starving good men to death.

Jake spent many silent hours contemplating what makes people of different races or nationalities hate each other enough to wage war. Perhaps, he conceded, the Bible did have an answer to this question, and to all his other questions, but since he had no Bible to consult, how would he ever know?

After Bob's death, Jake noticed a slight improvement in the conditions at the prison. Perhaps the guards didn't want everyone under their supervision to die after all. Two and a half cups of rice as well as the bowl of watery soup were now served to each man three times a day, along with a slice of bread at each meal. Sometimes this was accompanied by a cup of hot tea. What a luxury it was for Jake on those occasions to breathe in the aroma of the tea and feel the hot liquid flowing down his throat and into his stomach. Sometimes there would also be chunks of some kind of meat in the watery soup they were served. Jake did not care what kind of meat it was. Whatever it was, it had protein in it, and his body needed protein if he was going to live long enough to tell the world how the Japanese had treated the Doolittle Raiders they had captured.

Besides the improved food rations, another surprise awaited the four remaining airmen—books. Five books were handed out to the men: *The Son of God* and *The Spirit of Catholicism* by Karl Adams, *The*

Unknown God by Alfred Noyes, *The Hand of God* by William Scott, and the American Standard Version of the Bible.

As each prisoner read a book, he would pass it on to the next prisoner via one of the guards, who would slide it into the cell through the slot in the door. Jake read with gusto the books that were delivered to him. He even memorized a long poem, titled *The Pleasures of Hope,* from one of the books, and he would recite verses from it to the other three men during exercise time. But what Jake really wanted to get his hands on was the Bible. However, it was agreed that each man could have the Bible for three weeks before he had to pass it on to the next man. Of course, the officers went first, and being the only enlisted man, Jake had to patiently wait nine weeks before it was his turn to read the Bible.

From the moment the Bible was brought to his cell, Jake barely slept or put the book down. Despite the fact that the light in his cell was dingy and the Bible text small, the words seemed to leap off the page at him. Jake started with the Old Testament, reading it straight through, and then the New Testament. And then he reread it, and then he went back and read yet again those passages that piqued his interest.

What amazed Jake as he read was how the Old Testament foretold the New, how the two dovetailed together to tell the story of Jesus. Jake was also deeply touched by the accounts of Christ's suffering at the hands of the Jews and the Romans. As he spent time reading and rereading the Bible, Jake became aware of a presence in the cell with him. That presence, he concluded, was God right there beside him, reaching out to someone who was lost, alone, and abandoned. The feeling overwhelmed Jake: someone really cared about him. Someone wanted to lift a burden from him, lead him to a new life, and offer a new way of thinking and living.

On June 8, 1944, as Jake continued voraciously reading the Bible, he read Romans 10:9: "Because if thou shalt confess with thy mouth Jesus as Lord, and shalt believe in thy heart that God raised him from the dead, thou shalt be saved." Jake had already read the verse several times before as he read through the Bible, but this time the words seemed aimed right at his heart. He knew he had to respond to them. Right there in his cell in Nanking, China, Jake bowed his head and prayed. "Lord," he began, "though I am far from home and though I am in prison, I ask for Your forgiveness."

As he prayed, Jake was overcome by a strange sensation. Despite the fact that he was a prisoner of war in solitary confinement in a brutal Japanese prison in China, his heart was filled with joy—joy like he had never felt before in his life. And at that moment he would not have traded places with anyone. He knew he had received God's forgiveness. He was a new man. The horrors of prison life that surrounded him no longer had any sway in his mind. Nor did death. Death was merely something to be passed through on the way to eternity with Christ. Jake DeShazer was now God's man. It might not have looked to the Japanese guards that much had changed on the outside. Jake looked to them to be the same bedraggled American airman who had helped bomb their homeland over two years before. But on the inside, everything had changed. Everything was new and alive to Jake.

During the remainder of his three weeks with the Bible, Jake managed to memorize many long passages of Scripture, which he would recite aloud to himself.

It also wasn't long before Jake had an opportunity to demonstrate to himself and the others just how much he had changed on the inside. Jake was being escorted back to his cell after exercise one morning when the guard slapped his back and pushed him, yelling, "Hayaku! Hayaku!" (Hurry up! Hurry up!) When they reached Jake's cell, the guard pushed Jake roughly inside, slamming the cell door behind him and jamming Jake's bare foot in the door. Before he could do anything, Jake felt the thud of the guard's hobnailed boot against his bare heel. Excruciating pain shot up Jake's leg as the guard kicked his heel yet again. Finally Jake was able to wiggle his foot free and scurried to the far side of the cell while the guard turned the key in the cell door lock and walked away chuckling to himself.

Meanwhile, Jake sat in agony, cradling his throbbing foot in his hands. His first reaction to the guard's viciousness was anger and resentment and a desire to get revenge. But as he sat through the day and into the night reciting Bible verses aloud to himself that he had memorized and pondering Jesus' admonition for Christians to love and forgive their enemies, Jake knew that was what he had to do. Instead of seeking revenge for what the guard had done, he needed to forgive the man and reach out to him with love and respect.

The next morning when the guard came on duty and slid open the slot in the cell door to check on the prisoner, Jake said to him, "Ohayo gozaimasu!" (Good morning). Caught by surprise by Jake's greeting, the guard just stood and looked at Jake strangely. By the look on the guard's face, Jake decided that the guard must have thought he had gone mad from being cooped up in solitary confinement. But nothing could have been further from the truth. Rather than being mad, Jake felt totally in control of his actions. He genuinely meant what he had said.

The following morning when the guard came on duty, Jake once again greeted him with, "Ohayo gozaimasu!"

Day after day, Jake continued to greet the guard in the same manner, until one day the guard came to the cell door to talk to Jake. In the limited Japanese he had picked up during his time as a prisoner of war, Jake tried to have a conversation with the guard. He asked the guard how many brothers and sisters he had, and he asked him about his wife and children. He learned that the guard's mother had died when the guard was young, and that the guard prayed to his mother regularly as was the manner of the Japanese.

A rapport began to develop between guard and prisoner, and a few mornings later the guard again showed up at Jake's cell door. As Jake went over to talk to him, the guard slipped a cooked sweet potato through the slot in the cell door. Jake was both surprised and delighted by the guard's action. He thanked the man profusely for the sweet potato and then sat down in the corner to devour it. Nothing he had eaten in a long while tasted as good as the boiled sweet potato did at that moment. As he ate, Jake marveled at how following the Bible's lead to love and forgive his enemies had indeed changed the situation between him and the guard.

Chapter 12

In God's Hands

Over the next few weeks, the guard brought Jake fried fish and some candy to eat. As he had with the sweet potato, Jake relished them, thanking the guard and God for their provision for him.

As the wretchedly hot summer gave way to fall and then to another harsh winter, Jake continually repeated to himself the memorized Bible passages. It was a joy to him to have something positive to think about and dwell on. But despite Jake's new rapport with the guard, the guards were still capable of meting out harsh treatment to the prisoners.

The winter of 1944–1945 brought record snowfall to Nanking, and the snow lay on the ground until March. As a result, during their exercise time outside, the four airmen would have to run to stay warm. But to run they needed to take off the slippers they wore when outside and run in their bare feet in the snow. They were not supposed to take off their slippers when outside, but mostly the guards turned a blind eye to the infraction. However, during one such exercise period, a guard became incensed that the prisoners had taken their slippers off. He ended the exercise time early and told the airmen to return to their cells. Normally the men washed off their feet at a spigot before putting their slippers back on. But when George Barr came to wash his feet, the guard refused to let him do so. Instead, the guard tried to push him away. George angrily spun around and elbowed the guard in the stomach.

The surprised guard called for help, and the other three airmen were dispatched to their cells. As they were going, guards came running with a straight-jacket. Jake turned back to look and saw about ten guards surrounding George, rough handling him into the straightjacket. Jake cringed at the sight. From the time he had been captured, George had been picked on and taunted by the Japanese. George was a tall, lanky redhead, something most Japanese had never seen before. To them he was an oddity in a culture that emphasized the value of blending in and not standing out. As a result, the Japanese guards seemed to mark out George for much harsher treatment than the rest of the men.

Back in his cell, Jake waited anxiously. He could not see what the guards were doing to George, but he could tell from the screams that reverberated around the prison that George was in serious trouble. George's screaming went on for an hour before it subsided into low groaning. Jake waited impatiently for a Morse code message on his cell wall telling him that George was all right. Finally the message came, and Jake breathed a sigh of relief.

On November 15, 1944, Jake added up the years. It was his thirty-second birthday. He knew that his mother and stepfather would be praying for him, especially today, and now for the first time he also felt linked to them in prayer. It was a great comfort to Jake to know that he was spiritually linked with his family, even though time and distance separated them.

A little over five weeks later it was Christmas Day, and although the routine and food in the prison remained the same, the Doolittle Raiders were in for a wonderful Christmas treat. Jake sat in his cell wondering what his family back home in Oregon were doing for Christmas. As he contemplated the Christmas dinner they were probably eating, Jake became aware of a distant roar that began to get louder and louder. Suddenly he realized that it was the sound of airplanes. He quickly jumped to his feet and positioned himself to see the tiny patch of sky through the window high on the wall of his cell. To Jake's amazement, moments later a group of shiny silver fighter planes zoomed overhead. Jake had no idea what kind of planes they were, but there was no doubt that they were American planes. Jake could hardly contain his excitement.

Moments later Jake heard the sound of machine-gun fire and then the percussive boom of bombs exploding. As quickly as he could, with hands and feet against opposite walls, Jake worked his way up the ten feet to the window to see what was happening. To his delight he could see black smoke billowing from some oil storage tanks and an oil refinery in the distance.

As he watched the smoke rise from the oil tanks, Jake found himself thinking back thirty-two months before as he and his crewmates in the *Bat* bombed similar oil storage tanks in Nagoya, Japan. Many horrors had been visited on him since that time, but Jake did not regret his involvement in the Doolittle Raiders attack on Japan.

As soon as Jake had climbed down from his perch by the window, he began tapping a Morse code message to the cell next door. It was hard for the four airmen to contain their excitement as a flurry of Morse code messages passed between them.

Despite his excitement, Jake felt a certain apprehension, one he was sure he had in common with his fellow imprisoned Doolittle Raiders. The war might be close to ending, but what would happen to them? Every guard who talked about it said the same thing: the remaining Doolittle Raiders would never be handed over to the Allies; they would be executed first. Did the possibility of the war ending mean liberty for the men, or did it mean death? It was a question no one could answer.

Several weeks before, a guard had told Jake and the others that the Japanese had captured New York and San Francisco and that it would be only a matter of time before they controlled the whole of the United States. Jake and the others had dismissed this news as propaganda. Now, from the dejected look on the guards' faces, Jake decided that the guards believed their own stories. They had obviously not been expecting such an attack by American planes. And despite the clear evidence of billowing black smoke that choked the sky over Nanking, the guards tried to tell the airmen that all the American planes had hit with their bombs was the river, where they had killed some fish. The guards' reaction demonstrated once again their blind devotion to the invincibility of the emperor and Japan. It seemed impossible for them to really contemplate the idea that Japan would be beaten and forced to surrender.

Despite the excitement of the Christmas Day raid on Nanking, nothing more out of the ordinary happened during the next six months as Jake and the others shivered their way through another unusually cold winter, which to their relief eventually gave way to a moderate spring. Then on June 15, 1945, at six thirty in the morning, Jake and the other three men were told to hurry from their cells. They were handcuffed and shackled and then engulfed in large green raincoats. A guard placed a hat on Jake and rolled a mask down over the front of it so that he could not see. Then the men were roped together and told to march—where to, Jake did not know.

Two hours later Jake found himself sitting in a train carriage. He could not see from behind the mask, but he could hear people talking in Japanese, and he could feel the train swaying along the track. As the day got hotter, Jake recoiled from the odor of a hundred people in close proximity.

The masks were taken off at noon, and Jake looked around. The carriage was filled with Japanese people, many of them men in uniform, though there were also many women sitting on luggage piled in the aisle. Jake was glad to see that his three fellow Doolittle Raiders were still with him.

Food was bought to the prisoners—meat and rice—and it tasted delicious. All that was needed was a cup of tea to wash the food down, but it did not materialize. Instead, the mask was put back on, and Jake was left to take in the sounds and smells of the journey.

The procedure at lunch was repeated at dinner. And again, curiously, there was not anything to drink with the meal. The next morning there was more food, but still nothing to drink. By now Jake had a terrible headache and asked his guard for water.

The guard just laughed and said, "The more liquid we give you, the more you will have to be escorted to the latrines. No liquid, no latrines!"

Jake groaned. How bizarre it was to be finally getting some good food, only to have to worry about passing out from dehydration.

The journey lasted for three long, dry days. By the end of the journey the men were so weak that they had to be helped down from the train. Once off the train, one of the guards announced that they were now in Peking. Jake wished he had paid more attention to geography in school. He was not exactly sure where in China Peking was, though from the position of the sun in relation to the train during the trip he had figured out that they were traveling in a northerly direction.

Later that day the four airmen found themselves back in solitary confinement in yet another military prison. Jake wondered why the Japanese had made the effort to move them out of Nanking. Whatever way he looked at it, as far he was concerned, it turned out to be a poor move. The Nanking prison guards could be cruel, although some of them showed their human side at times, whereas the guards at the prison in Peking were all business. New horrors awaited Jake when he entered his cell. Inside were a woven mat, a single blanket, and a low stool about eight inches long and four inches wide.

"Sit down and face the wall," the guard instructed. "And don't move or look around. You will be punished if you do so."

Jake sighed as he perched himself on the stool and faced the brick wall of the cell. He did not dare move his body, but after a while he moved his head very slowly so that he could see the rest of the cell.

Jake soon learned that he was expected to stay sitting on the stool facing the wall for sixteen hours a day, except when eating the three meager meals that were served to him or when using the benjo. Sitting still for that long was its own kind of torture, and as he endured the sixteen hours on the stool, Jake recited the many Bible passages he had memorized.

Jake's only relief was knowing that Bob Hite was in the adjoining cell. Sometimes at night Bob and Jake could talk to each other through the benjo, since the pipes from the two toilets were connected to each other. If Jake got down close to the hole and spoke loudly, Bob could hear him, and vice versa. Of course, they were taking a risk in communicating this way. They had no idea what the punishment for talking through the benjo might be, but it was a risk that was worth taking to hear another friendly voice.

The days went by, and no one came to take Jake out of his cell for exercise, though once a week the four Doolittle Raiders were allowed a bath. This was their only opportunity to check on how the others were doing. When the men did get together, Jake was alarmed by the deterioration in George Barr's health. Because of George's height, red hair, and freckles, the guards constantly picked on him. And now it appeared to Jake that George was near death. Sometimes George lay unconscious while the others took their baths.

Jake realized that he was not far behind George. He had developed a severe case of dysentery, and boils had once again erupted all over his body, even on the soles of his feet. There were many times that Jake would have cried with the pain from the boils, if he'd had the energy to do so. The nights were unbearably long; sleep was fitful and interrupted by screaming and moaning throughout the jail.

After a month of agony, Jake knew that he could not go on sitting on the stool hour after hour each day. He felt like his heart was beating so slowly and erratically that it could stop at any moment. He began to pray about his predicament, and as he prayed, the story of Daniel came to mind. He remembered how King Darius had cast Daniel into a den of lions and how in the midst of the lions Daniel had knelt and prayed and God had shut the lions' mouths so that they did not attack and kill Daniel. Without hesitation, Jake slipped off the stool and knelt in front of the cell door, his hands folded in prayer. Whatever happened next, as far as he was concerned, he was in God's hands.

A guard came by and peered into the cell. When he saw Jake on his knees facing the door, he beat on the cell door with his sword and ordered Jake to get back on the stool and face the wall. But Jake continued praying, even though he knew it was against prison rules for anyone to so much as look at the door. Jake heard the guard walk briskly away and then return a minute or so later with several other guards.

The cell door swung open, and Jake braced himself for the beating that was sure to follow. But there was no beating. Instead, the guards walked around Jake, as if they were amazed at what he was doing. Then, without saying a word, they left and returned a short time later with a medic. The medic laid Jake on the woven mat on the floor. He then knelt down beside Jake and gave him a shot of medicine, after which he told the guards to leave Jake alone to rest.

It felt heavenly for Jake to be off the stool and free to lie down. Even better news was to follow. At mealtime Jake thought he was hallucinating. On the enamel plate that was slid through the slot in the cell door were boiled eggs, nutritious bread, and thick vegetable soup. And then a guard handed Jake a pint of milk to wash down the meal. While the medicine and the food made Jake's body stronger, it was Jake's faith that was bolstered the most through the experience. Even in the midst of prison, Jake now knew that God was always with him, looking after him and giving him strength to go on.

Several weeks later, on August 9, 1945, something even more astonishing happened for Jake. He awoke on his woven mat on the cell floor in the morning with the distinct impression that he should pray for peace. Not at some time in the future but right then and there! Jake started to pray as hard as he could. He asked God to put a great desire in the hearts of the Japanese leaders so that they would want to end the senseless war.

Throughout the entire morning Jake prayed, and through lunchtime as well. Then at around 2:00 PM he felt God tell him, "You can stop now. You don't need to pray anymore. The victory is won."

Jake was ecstatic upon hearing this. Nothing had changed on the outside, but Jake was 100 percent sure that the war was over. Now all that the captured Doolittle Raiders had to do was wait for word of the end of the war to reach Peking.

Jake pretended he needed to relieve himself and limped over to the benjo. No guard appeared to be watching, so he bent down and talked into the toilet pipe. "Bob, Bob, are you there?"

"What's wrong?" came Bob's reply.

"Nothing. I can't tell you everything, but I was praying, and it was revealed to me that the war is over today and we are victorious."

"That's great, Jake," Bob replied in an astonished voice. "I sure hope so."

"I know so!" Jake said jubilantly. "We just have to wait for rescue now."

As time went on and Jake was mysteriously given more meager but nutritious meals and more medicine, he felt himself growing stronger by the day. He refused to entertain the thought that he would be killed rather than freed by the Japanese. Instead, Jake's thoughts turned to what he would do when he was released. This was something new for Jake. Until this point he had not felt confident that that day would come. Now he was sure the release was just days away. As he contemplated his release, Jake promised God that he would thank his mother and stepfather for his godly upbringing.

Eight days later Jake stared at the tiny window high in the brick wall above him. Smoke billowed in the distance, and pieces of burned paper fluttered around in the air. The guards who brought dinner were wearing new uniforms. Jake was sure that they had broken into the supply cupboard and stolen the uniforms—another sign that the end of war had happened and that Japanese military discipline was breaking down.

That night seemed like one of the longest nights Jake had ever experienced. This time, though, it was not because he was despairing. No, he was too elated to sleep. His body was still in pain and he was hungry, but he knew it would not be long now.

He lifted up his hands and said, "Lord, take me. I just want to leave this suffering and be with you." Then he became aware of his hands. They were empty and Jake thought, "I can't go like this." He wanted more time to serve the Lord. He was a shy public speaker, but maybe he could at least be a church janitor. He said, "Lord, I don't want to come to you with empty hands. Give me another chance and I'll try."

As Jake passed the long night, his mind drifted to what Japan would be like after the war. In prison he had seen how the soldiers worshiped and obeyed their emperor as if he were a god. What would happen when the emperor surrendered, leaving the Japanese without the assurance that they were invincible?

Suddenly Jake sat bolt upright. It was as if the air around him were electrified. Then he heard a voice speak to him: "You are called to go and teach the Japanese people and go wherever I send you."

Goose bumps rose on Jake's arms as he tried to take in the experience. Was it real? Had God spoken to him that the war was over? And was God now commanding him to return to Japan? But as what? A missionary?

The idea astonished Jake, but he determined not to dismiss it.

Chapter 13

Senso Owari

On the evening of August 20, 1945, Jake was settling in for another long night in his cell when
without warning, the cell door swung open. A guard
was standing outside. "Come with me," he ordered.

Jake stepped tentatively out of his cell, just in
time to see Bob and Chase emerge from their cells.
Then George Barr, propped up by two guards, was
brought out of his cell. The men were marched to a
room they had never been in before—a room with a
faucet and a mirror.

"Time to shave," one of the guards said. "And we
will give you haircuts if you like."

The guard's statement seemed so foreign to Jake.
The airmen were being given a choice as to whether
or not they wanted haircuts. It was the first choice

Jake had been offered throughout three years and four months of incarceration in Japanese military prisons. And more surprises followed. Hot water came out of the faucet when the tap was turned on, a luxury Jake had last enjoyed back onboard the USS *Hornet*. As he shaved, Jake decided that he did not want a haircut—or what amounted to a head shaving. Perhaps—he hardly dared hope this—but perhaps they were going home, and he wanted to look as normal as possible.

Looking in the mirror, Jake realized that his wavy brown hair was probably one of the few things any of his family would recognize. Scars from various infections lined his now gaunt, pale face, his cheeks were sunken, and his bright blue eyes seemed unnaturally large.

When Jake had finished shaving, it was George's turn. Since George was too weak to hold his head up, one of the guards held his face while the other shaved him.

Next, Jake was handed an American Army Air Corps uniform to change into. It took him a moment to register that it was his old uniform, which he gladly put on, even though it was now two sizes too large for him.

When the men had all washed, shaved, and changed clothes, they were marched into the courtyard. George, weakened from being shaved, was loaded onto a stretcher and carried out. A prison official was waiting for them in the courtyard. "*Senso owari*—the war is over. You can go home now," he announced, bowing to the captured Doolittle Raiders. His words took a moment to sink in, and then the three prisoners embraced. Tears streamed down their cheeks. Somehow they had survived and were now going home. It was too much for them to fully take in after forty months in prison, with all but 184 days of that time spent in solitary confinement.

The next few hours were a blur to Jake. There were so many sights and sounds to try to make sense of. A truck arrived at the prison to take the men to a former luxury hotel in the heart of Peking called the Grand Hotel des Wagons. For the first time since being captured, the airmen were allowed to roll up the canvas sides of the truck and see the outside world. What a sight it was! Hundreds of Chinese men and women swarmed around them waving flags and singing in celebration of the liberation of their country. Jake tried hard to concentrate on what he was seeing, but it was hard to think through the past few hours and all that it really meant.

Once inside the hotel, the men were ushered to the dining room. At one end of the room two Chinese women were spooning something onto plates. Like magnets Jake, Bob, and Chase were drawn toward the food the women were serving. It turned out to be hearty Irish stew, full of pieces of lamb and chunks of vegetable. Irish stew had never smelled or tasted so good to the men as they ate heartily.

During the meal, the three men were informed that George had been taken straight upstairs to a makeshift hospital ward on the fourth floor, where he was being treated with intravenous drugs. Following the meal, Jake and the other two men were ushered into another room, where they were given quick physicals, vitamin shots, and pills.

Even after their hearty meal and physicals, Jake found it difficult to grasp the fact that he was actually free and talking to other Americans and to Englishmen, Canadians, and Dutch men and women who were now liberated from Japanese internment camps. These camps had housed civilians who had been stuck in China when the war broke out. But unlike the captured Doolittle Raiders, they had had access to Red Cross parcels and even mail sometimes, and for the most part they were much healthier than Jake and the others.

Sometime in the course of the evening's events, Jake was told that their names and serial numbers had already been wired back to the United States and that news of their release would be broadcast over American radio stations within minutes. Jake tried to picture his mother hearing his name over the radio. Then, in a moment of panic, he wondered whether she was still alive. He tried to push the thought aside and concentrate on the news that those at the hotel were telling him. The war had officially ended five days ago, on August 15, 1945, but it had taken five days for the Japanese to admit that they still had the captured Doolittle Raiders imprisoned.

Jake wondered about the significance of August 9, when he had prayed and felt God telling him that the war was over. He soon found out that on that date an

American B-29 Superfortress bomber had dropped an atomic bomb on the city of Nagasaki. This was the second such bomb the Americans had dropped on Japan. Three days before, on August 6, an atomic bomb had been dropped on the city of Hiroshima. The two bombs had devastated their targets and ended Japanese resistance to a peaceful surrender to the Allies.

That night the three airmen were assigned a room on the fifth floor of the hotel. As they climbed the stairs to their room, they had to sit down at each landing to catch their breath and gather their strength before continuing the climb. But the climb was worth it. In the room three beds awaited them.

Jake had to admit that it had been one of the strangest days of his life as he breathed deeply and lay down on the bed. He was free, his stomach was full, his body was cradled in a soft mattress, and there were no lightbulbs glaring overhead throughout the night. It felt like heaven to him.

For the next three days Jake struggled with all of the information the others at the hotel tried to tell him. They were eager to fill him in on how the war had been won, which battles were decisive, and what they thought would happen next. All that they told him was interesting, but Jake's mind was focused on just one thing—getting home and seeing his family.

On the morning of August 24, 1945, Jake, Bob, and Chase were flown out of Peking on the long journey back to the United States. An American doctor had evaluated George and declared him unfit to travel with them, a decision that made Jake and the others sad. The four airmen had come so far together, and now one was separated from the rest of the group.

Their first stop on the trip home was Chungking, China, where news reporters interviewed the men. Jake was happy to talk about his new faith and announced that he planned to return to Japan as a missionary. The reporters seemed to find this astonishing and questioned Jake from many angles.

In Chungking, Jake learned that he had been promoted in rank from corporal to staff sergeant and had been awarded the Distinguished Flying Cross and the Purple Heart for his part in the Doolittle Raid.

Following the news conference, the army officially debriefed the three Doolittle Raiders. Army officers wanted to know all of the details about their time in captivity and what exactly had happened to Will Farrow, Harold Spatz, and Dean Hallmark. They told Jake that they were collecting evidence for war crimes trials against the cruelest of the Japanese prison guards and overseers. Jake told them all he could think of, though it was difficult for him to sort through the jumble of his thoughts and feelings and put events in the right order. Although he realized the importance of the debriefing, more than anything Jake wanted to get home.

When they had finished debriefing the three airmen, the army officers told Jake and the others that in the three months following their raid on Japan the Japanese had ruthlessly killed a quarter of a million Chinese men, women, and children. The Japanese had done this in retaliation against the Chinese civilians who had helped many of the Doolittle Raiders to safety. As he listened to the depressing story, Jake wondered how much the world had changed while he'd been imprisoned. Had the United States been attacked? What was left of Japan and Germany? But he felt too confused to try to piece together the answers to these questions just yet.

Following their time in Chungking, the three Doolittle Raiders were on their way again. There were more stops and delays along the way, but on September 5, 1945, the plane carrying them touched down at Bolling Field, outside Washington, D.C. As he stood on the tarmac, Jake marveled at the fact that he was back in the United States. He had sometimes wondered during his forty months of imprisonment whether he would ever see his homeland again. And now here he was, his feet firmly planted on American soil.

The first thing Jake did once he got home was to call his parents. To his great relief, both his mother and his stepfather were still very much alive and doing well. They had sold the farm at Madras and retired to Salem, Oregon. Jake could tell that his mother was overwhelmed at hearing his voice, and she broke down crying on the phone. Jake assured her that he would be home just as soon as he could.

From Bolling Field the three men were transported to Walter Reed Military Hospital, where they were all given thorough medical checkups. And there were more press interviews. Jake was astonished to learn that although over 125,000 other American POWs were being released from Nazi and Japanese prisons, the sacrifices of the Doolittle Raiders had made a deep and lasting impression in the hearts and minds of the American public.

Jake also learned that three movies—*Thirty Seconds Over Tokyo, The Purple Heart,* and *Destination Tokyo*—had been made about the daring raid on Japan. Some of Hollywood's most famous stars had played parts in the movies, from Cary Grant to Spencer Tracy and Robert Mitchum. The movies ranged from the factual to pure fiction, but they had all helped to boost the morale of the American people during a desperate time. Jake could hardly believe the amount of press coverage the whole Doolittle Raid had generated. Articles about the raid had appeared in *Life, Time, Reader's Digest,* and *Colliers* magazines.

Jake read slowly through one of the old magazine articles to learn what had happened to his fellow raiders. He read that all but one of the Mitchell B-25 bombers that had taken part on the raid had ditched in China and the other plane had landed in Russia. After various harrowing adventures, sixty-four of the Doolittle Raiders had made their way to Chung-king, which was still under Chinese control. From there they had been returned to the United States, where most of the men were able to continue fighting in the war. One of the Raiders, Corporal Leland Faktor, the gunner/engineer of plane #3, had been killed bailing out of his plane, and sergeants Donald Fitzmaurice and William Dieter had died after the crash landing of the *Green Hornet* into the ocean. The crew who had landed in Russia had been detained but not imprisoned by the Soviet government. And the Japanese had captured eight of the Raiders. The article stopped there, but Jake knew the ending: three of the eight were executed by their captors, one died of starvation while in prison, and four came home.

Finally, the American public were told the ending to the story, and they were eager to hear every detail. Jake was paid $2,250 to tell his story for newspaper syndication, and a radio show paid him $400 for reading a one-sentence endorsement on the air.

Jake was given nine weeks' leave from the army. It was time to go home to Oregon to see his family. Jake stared out the airplane window as the majestic Rocky Mountains spread north and south below him as far as he could see. What a wonderful sight it was! As he flew west, Jake thought about his future. He was a Christian now, he knew that for sure, but what did this mean now that he was a free man? While in prison he had learned how to love his prison guards and how to pray, but what kinds of things had to change now that he was out of prison and back home in the United States?

As Jake sat contemplating these questions he felt God speak to him: "I don't want you to touch alcohol or tobacco ever again." Jake was not surprised. His Church of God upbringing had been strict about such matters, and Jake was sure that many ex-servicemen would turn to alcohol for comfort and solace. He did not want to be one of them. Right there, sitting on the plane flying over the Rocky Mountains, Jake made a vow to keep away from consuming alcohol and smoking for the rest of his life.

When Jake arrived in Portland, Oregon, reporters and a military escort met him at the airport. The army wanted to make sure that Jake came home in style. The group arrived at his parents' home in Salem around midnight—several hours later than expected. His mother and stepfather and many of his siblings and their families were waiting for him. It was a joyful reunion, one that Jake had rehearsed a thousand times over during his forty months of imprisonment.

Of course, Jake was too excited to sleep that night, and he sat up talking to his mother, stepfather, and half sister Helen. His mother told him the story of how her faith had been kept alive while the Japanese held him. "You had been gone several weeks when I woke up suddenly one night with a strange feeling that I was being dropped down, down through the air," his mother said. "I couldn't work it out, but I got the idea that it was something to do with you. So I started praying hard that God would take care of you. Eventually the burden lifted, and I was able to go back to sleep.

"Later I heard about the Doolittle Raid over Tokyo. Everyone did, but I had no idea you were involved until a reporter from the *Portland Journal* called us to find out about you and ask for a photograph. When we asked why he was interested in you, he said the paper had information that you were part of the

Doolittle Raid and had probably been taken prisoner. My heart dropped, because I knew how the Japanese treated their prisoners.

"I felt that same burden again many times, and all I could do was pray that God would surround you with His angels. I thought, *If my Jakie has angels to keep him company, he can't do better than that.*

"Then one day a US military officer came to the house with the terrible news that all the captured Doolittle Raiders had been executed by the Japanese. I told him, 'No, sir. I believe Jake is still alive. I have that from a higher power.' But still it was a struggle to keep believing that you were alive without hearing a single word from you for over three long years," she said, dabbing her eyes with the corner of her apron.

Jake later learned that when the war was over his stepfather was despondent. Alone in his berry garden he wept. "Bands were playing everywhere, and the whole country was having a party. But how could I celebrate when our Jakie wouldn't be coming home?" he said.

Jake's sister Helen also told him that there were many times when his mother and stepfather were unable to eat their dinner. Their mother would cook a hearty meal, put it on the table, and then pace the floor staring at it. "I wonder if Jake has anything to eat tonight," she would say, and suddenly everyone's appetite would evaporate. Often those at the dinner table just looked at their meal and then slipped off their chairs onto their knees and prayed that God would provide for Jake.

Now that Jake was home, everyone ate well. Jake's mother kept on hand a constant supply of Jake's favorite foods—apple pie and fried chicken. She was determined to make up for all the home-cooked meals he had missed while imprisoned.

Over the next few days hundreds of relatives, friends, neighbors, and church folk passed through the house. Some came to get Jake's autograph, while others just wanted to shake his hand. Many stayed to take part in family devotions and offer thanks to God for Jake's safe return. Sometimes, as he listened to his stepfather reading a chapter of the Bible, Jake marveled at how his heart had changed. What was once dull and boring was now alive and exciting.

Jake also spent time each day sorting through the pile of mail he received. Letters arrived from strangers who wanted to wish him luck or tell him about family member they had lost in the war. Dozens of catalogs came from Bible colleges all over the country, eager for a famous Doolittle Raider to attend their school. It was all a little overwhelming for Jake, who often would have to take a walk to clear his head.

A week after arriving back in Salem, Jake decided to make the 130-mile trip east to visit Madras, Oregon. The whole town of Madras gathered to celebrate Jake's homecoming, and Jake was asked to address the crowd. This was the first speech Jake had ever made in public, and his knees were shaking as he stepped forward to speak. At first his words were halting as he thanked the assembled crowd for the warm welcome and told them how good it was to be back among them in Madras. Then he began to tell them about his experiences as a prisoner of the Japanese and how in the midst of that he had responded to the gospel and how in an instant his life was changed.

The people listened attentively to what Jake had to say, but before too long he had run out of words. Nonetheless, Jake was encouraged. It wasn't the easiest thing he'd ever done in his life, but at least he had spoken publicly and openly about his experience. He felt that he could only get better at public speaking the more he did it. The opportunity to do more public speaking arose when Jake returned to Salem. He was asked to speak at a church service and at a youth rally. As he had done in Madras, he spoke from his experiences as a prisoner of war and explained the change becoming a Christian had made in his life.

Jake had been home in Oregon for only two weeks when a telegram arrived from the army, directing him to report immediately to the Santa Ana Air Base in California. No one could believe it. Jake was supposed to have nine weeks' leave. "Surely a man who has been a POW for so long deserves a longer break," his mother said in despair. But there was nothing anyone could do about the situation. Jake had not yet been discharged from the army, and he had no choice but to follow the orders he had been sent.

Jake packed his kit bag and set off for California to complete his army duty. Since the war was over, he had planned to ask for an immediate discharge upon his arrival at the Santa Ana Air Base. He was dumbfounded when his request for a discharge was denied because of a backlog of paperwork and because the whole discharge process was moving slowly.

There was not much for Jake or anyone else to do at the air base. Many of the men spent their days playing cards and drinking—but not Jake. He called on several of his Christian relatives in the area and set up speaking engagements.

Just as he was adjusting to this new phase of his life, Jake learned that he had been assigned to KP duty. One of the tasks given him was carrying trays of dishes to and from the mess hall to the kitchen. Jake, who had been liberated from the Japanese prison in Peking only a little over six weeks before, found the task to be physically draining. Still, he tried his best to load up the trays and successfully maneuver them where they needed to go.

One day while Jake was struggling with a tray of plates, he turned his head to catch the flash of a camera. An unauthorized newspaper cameraman had taken his photo. The next day everything broke loose at the air base. Jake's picture appeared on the front page of the *Los Angeles Times* with the caption, "Is this how America should treat a former POW and decorated war hero?" Apparently it was not, because later that day Jake was sent to the base hospital for observation, and the officer in charge of putting him on KP was given a severe reprimand. Within days Jake had his discharge papers from the army and was on his way back home to Salem, Oregon. He had $5,600 back pay in his bank account, and he was free at last. His days in the military were behind him.

A New Beginning

Jacob, this is President Watson," his sister Helen said as the two of them greeted a middle-aged man with caring eyes.

Jake smiled shyly.

The two men shook hands and President Watson said, "Your sister tells me that you are interested in attending Seattle Pacific College. Is that right?"

Jake did not quite know what to say. How could he explain to the president that he wasn't sure what kind of student he would make? Yes, he did want to be a missionary to Japan, and yes, he did know he would have to get some qualifications. But he had graduated from a tiny, rural high school nearly fourteen years before and had spent most of World War II in solitary confinement in a Japanese military prison.

157

As a result, he sometimes found it difficult to get his thoughts together and nearly impossible to speak them in the right order. He replied, "I'm thinking about making a slow start. Maybe taking a class or two next semester to see whether or not I can fit in."

President Watson took Jake's arm. "Are you sure that's a good idea?" he asked with a frown. "If God has called you to Japan, the sooner you get trained and over there, the better. The door is wide open now, but it might not always be that way."

Jake nodded. He'd had the same thought. But how, he wondered, could he settle into a rigorous college life just two months after being released from prison?

"Don't worry," President Watson assured, seeming to read Jake's thoughts. "There are plenty of people here to help you along. And besides, since you've been through military basic training, you already have some credits. That will lighten the load during the first year if you want." He looked directly at Jake. "The best thing is to jump straight in before you get sidetracked. The semester started two weeks ago, but we have a place for you, and the other students could help you catch up. It wouldn't be too difficult. I know everyone would welcome you here and do whatever they can to get you started."

Jake took a deep breath. He felt as though he were about to climb onto a roller coaster and strap himself in for the ride. Apparently President Watson and Helen, who served as Mr. Watson's secretary, had talked the situation out and believed that he could do it.

As Jake thought about it, something clicked inside him. Jake felt a surge of confidence. "All right," he said. "If you think I can do this, sign me up. I'll go home and talk to my parents and be back to start college tomorrow."

Jake drove home from Seattle to Salem in a state of shock. Only three months before he had been so ill in prison that he thought he was going to die. Now, as impossible as it seemed, he had just enrolled in college. The GI Bill would cover the cost of his college tuition and textbooks, and Jake felt confident that God was guiding him forward.

Back home Jake's mother was delighted when she learned of his new plan, though she made him promise that he would come home often to visit. She explained that she loved to hear his voice around the house and watch him eat and enjoy himself.

The next morning Jake packed up his few belongings and headed back to Seattle Pacific College. When he reached the campus, he discovered that news of his enrollment had traveled fast. All of the other students knew his name and who he was, and many of them came up to shake the hand of a Doolittle Raider and welcome him to the college. This new celebratory status took a little getting used to for Jake. He wanted to blend in and be just another student, but he knew that would not be possible. For one thing, every weekend Jake found himself out talking at Youth for Christ rallies or church services. Sometimes he teamed up at these events with the College Singers from Seattle Pacific College; at other times he went to them alone.

Although other students at Seattle Pacific College were usually asked to deliver sermons at meetings, everyone seemed to want Jake to tell the story of his captivity at the hands of the Japanese. At first Jake stumbled over his words and spoke in a monotone, but the crowds who came to hear him didn't mind. They took into account the lack of social contact he had suffered during the war. And when he ran out of things to say, Jake would recite many chapters of Scripture from memory. The crowds loved this as well because Jake spoke with such conviction. Yet aware of his need to become a better speaker, Jake enrolled in a speech class at college.

On the USS *Hornet*, before taking off to bomb Japan, Jimmy Doolittle had promised the men that he would throw a party for them once the mission was over. It had taken a while, but now that the war was over, Doolittle decided it was time for the party. In the fall of 1945, he arranged for the surviving Doolittle Raiders to gather for a party and a reunion at the MacFadden Deauville Hotel in Miami, Florida. Jake, though, was too busy with studying and speaking engagements to attend the reunion.

Interest in the exploits of the Doolittle Raiders was further kept alive in February 1946, when the US government brought a group of former Japanese prison guards and military officials to trial on a number of charges relating to their treatment of the captured Doolittle Raiders. The trial was held in Shanghai, and Chase Neilson returned to China to testify at the trial. Jake was not surprised that Chase was the one called on to testify at the trial. Throughout their time in prison, Chase had been driven by a strong desire to survive in order to be able to tell what happened to the captured Doolittle Raiders during their internment and to see that justice was brought and that those who had mistreated them were brought to trial and made to pay for their actions.

Jake had no doubt that his former tormentors would receive a fair trial—unlike the Japanese trial of the captured Doolittle Raiders. As the trial progressed, Jake found himself thinking about those prison guards on trial who had shown him kindness during his imprisonment. He wrote letters to the tribunal trying the guards in Shanghai and asked for leniency for the men. He explained that they had all been part of a system during the war that they could do little about. He was relieved when he learned that none of those on trial for the treatment of the Doolittle Raiders received the death penalty. Instead, the convicted guards were sentenced to imprisonment with hard labor for periods between five and nine years.

Jake was glad that he had not been asked to go to Shanghai to testify at the trial. His focus was now on getting his degree as quickly as possible. Jake did not have difficulty with his course work at Seattle Pacific College. He made good grades by working hard and spending long hours in the study hall. It was there that he met a junior named Florence Matheny.

Florence was a vivacious woman and a dedicated student. Like Jake, she was a few years older than the average student at Seattle Pacific College. She had already graduated with a two-year degree in Iowa and had taught at a small public school during the war years. Then in the summer of 1945, Florence felt that God wanted her in full-time Christian service as a missionary, though she was not sure where. She also felt that God was directing her to attend Seattle Pacific College, and so she enrolled in the school.

The more time Jake spent with Florence, the more he felt relaxed around her, until he finally asked her to go with him to a Youth for Christ rally where he was to be the featured speaker. Florence agreed, and from that time on Jake and Florence were constant companions.

One day Florence told Jake that several weeks before starting at Seattle Pacific she had picked up a newspaper and read an article about the four Doolittle Raiders who had just been released from forty months of incarceration in a Japanese military prison. She also read how one of these men had become a Christian while in jail and how he wanted to return to Japan as a missionary after he had attended a Christian college. She had mused to herself as she read the article what a coincidence it would be if the man chose to attend Seattle Pacific College and she got to shake hands with him. Jake and Florence laughed together over the incident. Not only had Florence gotten to shake the man's hand—now she was dating him.

In May 1946, just before the end of the school year, Jake and Florence were secretly engaged. Soon afterward, Florence told a few close friends of the engagement but asked them not to tell anyone. The plan worked well until the end-of-the-year college outing, which included a ferry trip up to Victoria, British Columbia, and a picnic in the seaside park there. Jake's mother and niece came along for the trip, though his mother had no idea that he and Florence were a couple.

As the ferry pulled away from the dock and headed for Victoria, Jake's mother offered him some motherly advice. "Jakie, why don't you date that Florence gal? I think you two would be good together."

Jake looked downcast at the suggestion and said, "Why, Mom, she's really popular. She wouldn't have anything to do with me."

"Oh yes she would," his mother replied, poking him in the chest as she spoke. "You just don't think enough of yourself. You just have to march up to her and ask her out!"

Jake nodded. "I might try that if you think it would work," he said, trying to hold back a smile.

An hour later, as they sailed into Victoria Harbor, the ferryboat's Klaxon sounded and a voice came over the speaker system. "Hello, we have a special announcement to make on this spring trip," said a female voice, which Jake recognized immediately as Florence's roommate's voice. "We would all like to congratulate Jake DeShazer and Florence Matheny on their engagement."

A loud cheer went up from everyone on board. Jake's mother turned to him in mock indignation. "Jakie, you knew this all the time and you didn't tell me!"

Jake chuckled.

Three months later, on August 29, 1946, Jake and Florence were married in a Free Methodist church in Gresham, Oregon. Florence's former pastor performed the ceremony. It was a small wedding. There were still a lot of shortages following the war, and Jake could not buy a white shirt for the event. Instead he had to borrow one from his stepfather and wore it with the same brown suit that he often wore to speaking engagements. Florence wore a white dress and carried a big bunch of yellow roses.

The wedding reception of cake and punch was supposed to have been held outside, but when it started to rain, one of the church women offered her house as an alternative, and the wedding party walked there from the church.

Following the wedding, Jake and Florence drove back to Toddville, Iowa, Florence's hometown, where they received a warm welcome from Florence's parents and sisters and brother. As they drove along, Jake and Florence made plans for their future. Florence had a call to be a missionary, but she had not known where the Lord was calling her. Now she knew for sure that her place was beside Jake in Japan. It was an exciting prospect for them both.

At the end of World War II, American General Douglas MacArthur had been appointed Supreme Commander of the Allied Powers in Japan. Now MacArthur was calling for churches in the United States to send as many missionaries to Japan as possible. The country had a religious vacuum, and MacArthur believed that Christian missionaries were necessary to fill that void by bringing hope to the people, along with a new set of values necessary for the new emerging Japanese society. As a result, Jake was eager to get to Japan as soon as possible. He and Florence discussed how he could complete the summer study program and graduate in two years instead of the three years of study he had left.

Classes at Seattle Pacific soon started up again for the new academic year. This time Jake and Florence shared a small duplex on the edge of campus. They were a happy couple, working together for a common goal. As Jake continued to be a sought-after speaker at churches and youth rallies, Florence would accompany him to his engagements and tell the audience a little about her own call to the mission field.

By the end of March 1947, the couple received some good news. Florence was expecting a baby in the fall. Jake was going to be a father! Florence took time off from college to have the baby, but they worked out a study plan so that she and Jake could graduate together in the summer of 1948.

Paul Edward DeShazer was born on October 31, 1947. He was a big, round baby, with the same dimple on his chin as his mother. At nearly thirty-five years of age, Jake was a proud father. He marveled that he had such a wonderful wife, and now he was a real family man as well.

Jake and Florence were members of the Free Methodist denomination. Normally the Free Methodists required two years of "home service" before new graduates could leave for a foreign mission field. However, the denomination made an exception in the case of the DeShazers. Everyone agreed that the sooner Jake and Florence got to work in Japan, the better it would be.

For the DeShazer family the rest of the year passed in a whirl of study and making concrete plans to live in Japan. They read all they could on postwar conditions in Japan. Things sounded bleak there, and they were warned that they would not be able to find a proper house to live in. They would also have to take with them everything they needed for four years of missionary service.

The United States was still experiencing postwar shortages of its own, and it became quite a feat for Jake and Florence to gather everything the family would need to live in a foreign country for any length of time. Florence and Jake wrote and rewrote lists of household goods that they would need: blankets, sheets, towels, plates, and pots; personal items such as clothing, shoes, and toiletries; and other items such as furniture, hot plates, an oven, boxes of canned foods, milk powder, and other staples. Many of their friends and family members donated items on the list. Soon the DeShazers' living room had been transformed into a packing station as crates and barrels of belongings were sealed and labeled, ready for the trip to Japan.

During this busy period Jake did take the time to write down his experiences for the Bible Meditation League. He often spoke at the organization's meetings, and the leaders asked him to write about his experiences so they could be published in tract form. Jake could not have imagined the impact the few paragraphs he penned would have on his future.

The family visited Jake's parents as often as they could. Jake's mother loved to dote on Paul. But as the time grew near for the family to depart for Japan, some of Jake's brothers and sisters became concerned. They could not see why Jake and Florence had to go all the way to Japan when there was plenty of missionary work to be done at home. Jake's sister Julia was particularly upset about how he had been mistreated by the Japanese. She could not believe that he was going back to live among them.

Meanwhile, Jake's brother Glenn had recently bought a large tract of land in Madras, Oregon, and was irrigating the land for the first time. Land in Madras was still cheap, and irrigated lands held the promise of good returns. Glenn urged Jake to buy some land of his own in Madras, but Jake refused to spend a cent on buying land in Oregon. Even though he had some savings left and the land looked like a good investment, he was afraid that owning land would distract him from his missionary calling. Above all, Jake wanted to keep his focus strong.

In June 1948, Jake and Florence DeShazer graduated from Seattle Pacific College, with both receiving a bachelor of arts degree with a major in missions. Although they both still had some course work to finish the requirements of their degrees over the summer,

Jake was proud of the fact that he had worked hard and earned a four-year degree in just three years.

At the end of the summer, after completing their course work, Jake and Florence spent time traveling around the United States, telling people about the great need for the gospel that existed in Japan. Then it was time for Jake, Florence, and Paul to leave. The family traveled to San Francisco, where on December 14, 1948, they boarded the USS *General Miegs* for the trip to Japan.

As the ship made its way down San Francisco Bay and under the Golden Gate Bridge, Jake could not help but think of the time six and a half years before when he had stood on the deck of the USS *Hornet* and watched as they passed under the fog-shrouded Golden Gate Bridge. Then he had been an angry young bombardier off on a daring mission to make Japan pay for its raid on Pearl Harbor.

After the ship had left San Francisco Bay behind, Jake made his way to his cabin and wrote: "This time I am not going as a bombardier, but I am going as a missionary. Now I have love and good intentions toward Japan. How much better it is to go out to conquer evil with the gospel of peace!"

Chapter 15

Back to Japan

During the war, the USS *General Miegs* had been a troopship, but it was now being used to carry the first load of 150 Catholic and Protestant missionaries to postwar Japan. Since the vessel was a former troopship, its onboard accommodation was far from luxurious. The men were quartered on the opposite side of the ship from the women and children. Florence and Paul shared a cabin with eighteen other women and children. The days aboard were filled with a mixture of excitement and routine. Florence had to wait in line for her turn to use the washing machine to wash Paul's diapers and clothes. Each afternoon she and Jake continued their limited Japanese language study with a missionary who was far ahead of them in his ability to speak Japanese. To pass the time, some of the passengers gave lectures on various subjects.

Jake was particularly interested in the lecture on the history of Christianity in Japan. He was surprised to learn that St. Francis Xavier, a Roman Catholic missionary from Spain, had introduced Christianity to Japan in 1549. Over the next fifty years, St. Francis's followers claimed to have half a million converts. Over the years, however, local princes opposed and resisted the gospel. The conflict became increasingly violent and ended in a bloody massacre in 1638. Following the massacre, Christianity was banned from Japan, and for the next two hundred years the country shut itself off from the outside world. No Japanese citizen was allowed to travel abroad, and no foreigners were allowed to enter the country.

In 1854 Commodore Matthew Perry arrived in Japan with a fleet of American warships and forced the opening of Japan to the outside world. Five years later the first handful of American missionaries came to Japan. When the edict against Christianity was lifted in 1873, more foreign missionaries began arriving in the country.

These missionaries faced many challenges, but eventually Christianity began to take root in the country and churches began to sprout. The first Free Methodist missionary in Japan was Masatsuga Kakihara, a Japanese man who had studied at Greenville College in Illinois. In 1895 he began preaching the gospel in the remote fishing village of Fukuda on Awaji Island.

Two years later he was joined by Teikichi Kawabe, another Japanese man who had become a Christian while living in the United States and had then served as a pastor for three years in San Francisco. Teikichi was a dynamic evangelist, and under his leadership Free Methodist churches began to spring up around Japan, particularly in the Osaka area. A seminary was established in Osaka to train Free Methodist pastors.

The war, though, had been hard on Christians in Japan. Foreign missionaries were forced from the country, and the Japanese government exerted its control over the church, forbidding certain hymns and verses from the Bible to be read or sung in church. Of course, the Allied bombing of Japan had been hard on the church. Jake learned that nine Japanese Free Methodist churches, along with eight Bible school buildings and many parsonages, had been bombed beyond repair.

On the way to Japan, the USS *General Miegs* docked in Honolulu, Hawaii, for a day. In Honolulu Jake and Florence were met by the parents of a couple of their friends from Seattle Pacific College. The parents whisked Jake off to speak at a Christian meeting in Honolulu. As they drove to the meeting, Jake marveled that he was finally in the islands where the Second World War had begun for the United States. He recalled how angry he had felt when he learned of the bombing of Pearl Harbor and how that anger had motivated a drive to make the Japanese pay for their actions. Now he marveled that he was in Hawaii on his way back to Japan, not to extract revenge but to tell the people the greatest news Jake had ever heard—the gospel.

On Christmas Day they were at sea and approaching Japan. Paul was too young to get into the spirit of things, but everyone enjoyed watching the excitement of the older children when they spotted Santa arriving in a lifeboat.

At dawn on December 28, two weeks after setting out from San Francisco, the low, dark profile of an island came into view on the horizon. Jake and Florence stood on deck watching as the main Japanese island of Honshu grew bigger and bigger before them. It wasn't long before the USS *General Miegs* was sailing into Tokyo Bay and heading for the port city of Yokohama. As the ship approached the dock, Jake could see nothing appealing about Yokohama's dreary buildings, with their peeling paint and unlighted windows.

"Jake, we really don't know how to be missionaries," Florence said in a hoarse whisper. "What are we going to do now that we've docked?"

Jake put his arm around his wife. He had been pondering the same question. The couple stood there in silence for a few minutes, and then it was time for them to gather their belongings for disembarkation. They said good-bye to algl the new friends they had made aboard ship and then headed off down the gangway, Jake carrying Paul under one arm. They had nearly reached the bottom of the gangway when the ship's loudspeaker crackled.

"Is Jacob DeShazer here? Is Jacob DeShazer disembarking?" came a voice over the speaker.

As Jake waved his free arm in the air, a man with a movie camera made his way through the crowd toward him and Florence.

"Please, go back on board. I work for an American news company, and I need some footage of you. Other reporters and photographers are waiting for you in the dining room," the man said.

Jake and Florence turned around and headed back up the gangway as those going down stood to one side to let them pass.

Back on the ship Jake and Florence made their way to the dining room, where about thirty men, mostly Japanese, were waiting for them with pens, paper, tape recorders, and movie cameras ready. As soon as Jake stepped inside the room, the reporters began firing questions at him.

"Why are you returning to a country where the people held you prisoner and treated you badly?" one Japanese reporter asked in heavily accented English.

"God has called me to tell the Japanese people about Jesus," Jake replied.

"How did God call you?" another reporter asked through an interpreter.

"I read the Bible while I was in prison, and I discovered that the Bible is God's Word. Jesus is the Savior of all mankind. If the Japanese people will accept Jesus as their Savior, they will have the Light of Life, and the love of Jesus will control their lives," Jake responded.

"Why do we need Jesus now?" someone else asked.

Jake smiled. "That's an easy one to answer," he said. "I know that the Japanese are very educated people, but I don't think they know what happened two thousand years ago, so I am going to bring them up to date!"

The impromptu press conference aboard the USS *General Miegs* upon their arrival in Yokohama was the beginning of a love affair the Japanese press had with Jake and his family. The journalists and cameramen followed the DeShazer family from the ship and to a nearby rooming house that had been arranged as temporary accommodations for the family. Photographers snapped photos as Jake and Florence took off their shoes and entered the house.

Inside the rooming house it was freezing cold. Jake realized that all he had read about postwar Japan was true. There was very little food, heating oil, or wood in the cities. Devastation and desperation were all around them.

Two days after arriving in Yokohama, Jake and Florence experienced their first setback. Up until then, their son Paul had been a robust, strong toddler, but in the cold, barnlike rooming house he had caught a bad cold. He lay in Florence's arms, his eyes glazed, unwilling to be coaxed into eating or drinking.

Concern soon turned to alarm, and the DeShazers sought out the nearest US Army hospital. The doctor told them that for Paul to survive he would need special nursing care and to be in a warm environment.

With great reluctance, Jake and Florence left Paul in the hospital and returned to their rented dwelling.

The Free Methodist Church in Japan had set up a round of speaking engagements for Jake. Despite Paul's illness, it was decided that Jake should go ahead with the meetings. While Jake was away speaking, Florence would visit Paul each day at the hospital.

Jake's first speaking engagement was on Sunday, January 2, 1949. He spoke at two Free Methodist churches—one in the morning and the other in the afternoon—in nearby Tokyo. When he arrived at the first church in Tokyo, Jake was introduced to the Reverend Dr. Kaneo Oda. Dr. Oda was a native Japanese man who was also a graduate of Seattle Pacific College. He lived in Osaka and was currently the superintendent of the Free Methodist Church in Japan. Dr. Oda explained to Jake that he would be his interpreter at the two services. The crowds at the services were enthusiastic as they listened to Jake speak, and Dr. Oda turned out to be an excellent interpreter.

Still, it was a strange feeling for Jake that day to be standing in front of hundreds of Japanese people and telling them about his experiences while incarcerated for forty months in a Japanese military prison. Jake told the congregation that he was glad they were no longer shooting at him and that he was no longer dropping bombs on them!

Osaka, Japan's second largest city, located on the eastern coast of Honshu Island about 220 miles southwest of Tokyo, was to be the DeShazers' new home.

After a week in the hospital, Paul DeShazer was well enough to be discharged. On January 19, Jake and Florence were relieved to climb aboard a train with their son for the trip to Osaka. They were glad to be leaving behind the cold and drafty rooming house in Yokohama.

When the family reached Osaka, Mr. Yoshiki, whose son had been killed in the war, offered his son's upstairs rooms for Jake and Florence to live in. Soon afterward the family's belongings arrived from the United States, and the DeShazers moved into their new lodging. Jake set up the American oil stove he'd had shipped over to keep the place warm. Because there was no kitchen upstairs, Jake set several packing cases on their sides to make a counter on which Florence could prepare food and cook it on a hotplate. With the arrival of their furniture, Jake and Florence were able to sleep in a Western-style bed. The "bathroom" consisted of a hole in the floor of a tiny room.

Florence arranged all of their food items in her new kitchen and said a prayer of thanks for all of the cans of milk that they had shipped over. The milk would keep Paul healthy and growing. Other supplies, like oatmeal and flour, did not do well in the damp climate of Osaka and had to be used up fast. This was not a problem. All around the DeShazers, Japanese families were nearly starving to death. Japan simply could not produce enough food to feed the population after the devastating war. Jake and Florence found themselves giving away much of their food, confident that God would supply more when they ran out entirely.

As Jake, Florence, and Paul settled into their new surroundings, they often encountered journalists watching them. Almost every day some tidbit was reported in the newspaper about how the family was doing. When Paul poked his pudgy little fingers through a paper panel door, the incident was reported in the newspaper. News photographers snapped pictures of Jake and Florence taking Paul for a walk and of Jake inviting the neighbors to a nightly Bible class they had started in their home. The next day the photos appeared in the local paper.

It seemed that everyone in Osaka knew Jake. Every time Jake went out he was greeted by name. Former guards and military men introduced themselves to him on street corners, and women held up their children to watch as he walked by. Jake soon learned that this all had to do with the tract he had written for the Bible Meditation League back in the United States. The tract, titled *I Was a Prisoner of Japan*, had been translated and published in Japanese, and over one million copies had been distributed throughout the country. The Japanese people, it seemed, were eager to read about Jake and the change that his becoming a Christian had made in his life. Japan was at a crossroads. The country's defeat in the war, coupled with Emperor Hirohito's declaration on January 1, 1946, that he was not a god but merely a mortal man, had created a spiritual vacuum in the country. Despite the people's sacrifice, the old religions had failed Japan, and now many Japanese people were looking for a new religion that could bring meaning, purpose, and direction to their lives. Jake's tract seemed to be one of the things many had latched onto in this search.

While Jake continued to be in demand as a speaker at church services, he and Florence realized that their fame provided an opportunity to spread the gospel far beyond the church. They just didn't know exactly how to do this. So they regularly asked God to show them how they were supposed to go about doing it.

One of the most regular visitors at the DeShazers' new home was Kaneo Oda. One day, about six weeks after their move to Osaka, Dr. Oda arrived just in time to help Jake and Florence with a dilemma. They had received so many letters since arriving in Japan that the letters now filled a basket to overflowing. But neither Jake nor Florence knew enough Japanese to adequately read the letters and answer them. Dr. Oda pulled one of the letters out of the basket. He opened it and began to translate it aloud into English. "Dear Mr. DeShazer," he read. "My brother and sister were killed by the atom bomb dropped by the Americans. Both of my parents are also very ill from the fallout. I have had a great hatred for the American people, but when I read your tract, it made me think that there might be a better way for me to live out my days. Perhaps it is possible and even desirable to forgive our enemies. Could you send me any information you have on how to go about this? Thank you."

Dr. Oda picked up a second letter and opened it. "Today, after reading about you and your lovely wife in the newspaper, I feel that I must write to ask you if you will be visiting Tokyo. I would very much like to talk with you and hear your remarkable story firsthand. I was a prison guard during the war, and when I read your story I felt a great shame—something I have not felt before—for what happened to you. Can your religion explain why I should feel this way now?"

Dr. Oda folded the letters and carefully studied Jake's face. "I imagine the whole basket is filled with letters like these. I will take care of them. We must pray about the best possible way to use this opportunity."

Within a week Dr. Oda returned for a visit to the DeShazers. The basket was again half full of letters.

"I have been praying over the letters, and I think you have a unique opportunity here," Dr. Oda said. "I have never seen so much interest in Christianity expressed in Japan. We have an open door here, and we must walk through it. We need to work together to reach as many people as possible." He leaned closer to Jake. "I have asked to be temporarily released from many of my superintending responsibilities so that I can tour Japan with you and be your interpreter. This would be for an indefinite time, as long as people want to hear you speak. Of course, it depends on whether you are willing to travel with me for many weeks out of the year."

Jake gulped. It was hard to imagine that one of the most prominent men in their denomination in Japan would take on a servant role for him. But the suggestion also made sense. Jake did not know enough Japanese to speak alone before crowds, and it would be a long time before he could do so. Dr. Oda was one of the best interpreters in the country, and together the two men would make a great team.

That night after Paul was in bed, Jake and Florence discussed the opportunity. They agreed that conditions would not be suitable for Florence and Paul to travel with Jake. And yet with the kind of travel schedule that the letters seemed to indicate, Jake could be away for weeks at a time, leaving Florence alone with the baby. Still, for two Bible college graduates whose hearts burned for missions, their decision was not difficult to make. When they had married, they had both committed themselves to doing whatever it took to spread the gospel in Japan. And now a wide-open door to do just that had presented itself.

The next morning Jake visited Dr. Oda and told him to set up an itinerary—they were on their way to evangelize Japan!

Chapter 16

More to Do

Jake felt as though he had stepped into the middle of a whirlwind! True to his word, Kaneo Oda had set up a fast-paced itinerary for them both. Within two months of agreeing to go on the road with Dr. Oda, Jake had spoken in over two hundred places—churches, schools, town halls, public gardens, factories, and coal mines.

One of the most memorable of these events was held in the spring of 1949. The manager of a large theater in Osaka invited Jake and Florence to come and watch the newsreel of their arrival in Japan. The owner had also invited to the event all of the former Japanese prison guards that could be found. The meeting was unlike anything Jake had ever before experienced. Jake spotted several guards he knew in the crowd and was introduced onstage to Captain Kato, who had been the head guard at the Nanking prison, where Jake had been held captive.

The two thousand people in the theater were hushed as the two men stood together. Jake smiled and reached out his hand to Captain Kato. "We meet today in the presence of the God who loves and offers forgiveness to all mankind," he said. Captain Kato nodded and then wiped a tear from his cheek.

Another time, after speaking in a church one Sunday morning, a young woman came up to Jake. "I had every intention of killing you," she said through Jake's interpreter. "Ever since I read about you in the newspaper, I have wanted to kill you as revenge for my two brothers who were killed in the war. But now that I hear your message, I no longer wish you dead. Instead, I feel compelled to ask you more about this God you talk of." Jake invited the young woman to his home, and she joined the steady number of Japanese people coming to the house after work to participate in Bible studies or chat with the DeShazers.

On June 17, 1949, Jake was invited to travel to Tokyo to meet Prince Takamatsu. The prince was the brother of the emperor, and it was a great honor for Jake to be invited to visit with him. Jake had never met a prince before and wasn't quite sure what to do when he arrived at the royal residence. When Prince Takamatsu entered the room, Jake just put out his hand and shook the prince's hand. The prince welcomed him warmly, and after they had sat down, a servant brought a tray of tea and cakes, and together they sipped tea and ate cakes while they talked.

One of the first things Jake did was to express his thanks to the prince for the emperor's mercy in sparing his life by commuting his death sentence during the war. Jake then went on to share the gospel with Prince Takamatsu and tell him what it means to be a Christian. He also told the prince about his speaking tour of Japan and how he was speaking to between eight thousand and ten thousand people per week. Prince Takamatsu seemed to be genuinely impressed by all that Jake was doing in Japan. Jake's hectic pace of speaking engagements around the country continued throughout the fall and winter.

As 1949 rolled on, to the west, in China, the communists were slowly but surely taking control of that country. There were also many in Japan who embraced communism, seeing it as providing new hope and a new direction for Japan. This motivated Jake and many other missionaries to reach out to as many Japanese people as possible with the gospel before the people could be wooed away by the promises of communist ideology.

In October 1949, Jake wrote to the Free Methodist mission board in the United States:

One of the greatest blessings has been the ability to witness. Often we can go right into the Buddhist schools and ask for a decision to become Christian. Many people respond gladly.... At one school, I was made honorary principal. After speaking there two or three times the whole student body, together with the principal, decided to become Christians.

Mrs. DeShazer is holding regular classes for teenagers and youngsters. She uses felt-o-grams to help make the message clear. When the opportunity comes, we both go together in the automobile which you gave us to use. Big crowds come to listen and they usually show much enthusiasm for Christianity.

Two months later, on December 11, 1949, Florence gave birth to John Douglas DeShazer, another strong, healthy boy. Jake was delighted, both with his new son and with all that had been achieved during their first year in Japan. He and Florence sat down together at Christmas to count their blessings. Throughout most of the year, Jake had been out speaking to around eight thousand to ten thousand people per week, while Florence ran an effective Bible class in their Osaka home each evening. They also now had a new son, and Paul had remained healthy throughout the year. Paul enjoyed the Sunday school that Jake and Florence ran in their home, and he often sat with up to eighteen other small neighborhood children on a big red couch while Florence taught the class. In addition to all of this activity and the ongoing difficult task of mastering the Japanese language, Jake wrote a book about his experiences as a Doolittle Raider. Fifteen thousand copies of the book were printed.

Christmas gave way to New Year's Day 1950—the dawn of a new decade. Jake kept busy through January and February, although he was becoming increasingly concerned about the political situation in Asia. The region was still very unstable following the Second World War. On October 1, 1949, the communists had taken complete control of China and established the People's Republic of China. Now it was looking as though the Korean Peninsula was also about to fall into the hands of the communists. Despite General MacArthur's ban on communism in Japan, the ideology was making inroads. Jake was convinced that more had to be done to win the Japanese people over to Christianity, lest Japan also fall into the hands of the communists.

In late February, Jake decided to embark upon a forty-day fast, during which he ate nothing and drank only water. He still kept up his punishing travel and speaking schedule and his language study, along with long periods of prayer for the nation of Japan. This dramatic move on Jake's part made a great impression on the Japanese people. They knew that Buddhist priests prayed from time to time, but it was unheard of for a foreign missionary to show such outward concern for their souls.

Once the fast was finished, larger crowds began to gather to hear Jake speak, but Jake could not shake the feeling that there was some other key to reaching the country that had yet to be unveiled to him.

One morning, less than a week after the end of his fast, Jake opened the door of his home to find two men standing there. One of the men was a fellow American, Glenn Wagner, the chief representative in Japan of the Pocket Testament League. The other man was Japanese and about Jake's age.

Glenn introduced the man to Jake as Captain Mitsuo Fuchida. As Jake bowed to his visitors, as was customary in Japan, his mind raced with excitement. Mitsuo Fuchida was one of Japan's most prominent war heroes. He had led the 360-strong squadron of airplanes that had bombed Pearl Harbor and forced the United States to enter the war. Jake wondered what the man was doing at his door.

Soon the three men were seated upstairs, and Jake was listening to an astonishing story. He sat spellbound as Captain Fuchida told how he had become a Christian. Two events had led up to this. The first had come as a result of his having been asked to testify in the war crimes tribunals held at the end of the war. Captain Fuchida himself had not been charged with any crimes, but he had been asked to describe situations he had seen during the war. He told Jake that as he listened to the trials, he became obsessed with the idea that each nation treats its prisoners of war badly and that it was a terrible injustice that the losing side in the war had to be humiliated because of their treatment of prisoners of war. To prove the point, he had begun tracking down and interviewing Japanese soldiers who had returned to Japan after being held as prisoners of war in the United States.

Captain Fuchida told how he met with one Japanese soldier named Kanegasaki, whom he had known from early in the war. This soldier had been a prisoner of war at a camp on the Colorado/Utah border. Kanegasaki told Captain Fuchida how an eighteen-year-old girl named Peggy Covell had befriended the entire camp. Peggy had visited the camp every day and had done whatever she could to help the captured Japanese soldiers.

Eventually one of the prisoners had asked her why she was so kind to them. Peggy told the prisoner that it was because Japanese soldiers had killed her parents, who had been missionaries in Yokohama and had fled to the Philippines at the beginning of the war. When the Japanese overran the Philippines, her parents had been found with a small radio and were accused of communicating with the outside world. They were given a mock trial, at which they were convicted of the crime and afterward beheaded.

At first, Peggy had explained, she was bitter about losing her parents. But then her heart softened, and she realized that her parents would have forgiven the Japanese before they died and that she needed to do the same. So she asked God to bless the Japanese people, and she began to volunteer at the camp helping the Japanese prisoners of war.

Fuchida explained to Jake how he could barely respond to this behavior. Until that time he believed completely in the principle of *katakiuchi*, the Japanese notion of revenge. A good Japanese warrior who had been captured and was awaiting death prayed that he would be born again seven times, so that in each of the seven lives he could extract revenge from whoever it was that had killed him.

Nonetheless, hearing the story of Peggy Covell's kindness and humanity toward the Japanese prisoners of war had convinced Fuchida to give up his quest to prove that the military courts were unjust. Instead, Fuchida had focused on searching for the source of such pure love. Surely, he reasoned, that was what he and the rest of the Japanese people needed to stop the cycle of hatred and secure a peaceful future.

Not long after this experience, Captain Fuchida had been handed a copy of Jake's *I Was a Prisoner of Japan* tract at a railway station in Tokyo. The captain explained how he had taken the tract home and read it many times, marveling at how God could change hatred into love. He explained to Jake that this was the second event that had convinced him that the God of the Christians was real. As a result, he bought a Bible and began to read it.

The process of turning his life over to Christ, Fuchida explained, had been a slow one, partly because of his strong Buddhist heritage. Now Mitsuo Fuchida sat in the DeShazers' living room, asking Jake if they could pray together. Jake was struck by the enormity of the moment as he knelt beside Mitsuo Fuchida. These two men had once been on opposing sides: one the leader of the Japanese attack on Pearl Harbor, the first attack of the war on American soil, and the other a member of the Doolittle Raiders, who had been the first to bomb Japan. Yet here they were, kneeling together side by side, praying with love in their hearts toward each other. Before the two men parted, they both agreed to speak at a large evangelistic rally that the Pocket Testament League was planning at Central Public Hall in Osaka on May 14.

On May 14, 1950, Jake, accompanied by Kaneo Oda, made his way to the hall. When they arrived at their destination, Jake could hardly believe his eyes. A huge crowd thronged around Central Public Hall, struggling to get into the already packed auditorium, and the police were trying to restore order to the situation. As a result, the meeting was half an hour late in starting. When it did start, four thousand people were crammed into the hall, and another three thousand were listening outside on a public address system.

At one thirty in the afternoon, Glenn Wagner called the meeting to order. After the singing of some hymns and the distribution of copies of the Gospel of John to the audience, Jake was introduced. The crowd applauded loudly, and then Jake proceeded to tell the audience the story of his capture by the Japanese in China, his time in prison, and his conversion to Christianity and how that had changed his life. As Jake spoke, Kaneo Oda translated his words for the crowd. Jake ended his talk by declaring to the audience, "Now I love you as a brother in Christ. Come to know Christ now, this afternoon."

Once again the crowd applauded loudly. Then Glenn introduced Mitsuo Fuchida, and again the crowd went wild with applause. This was their war hero, and this was the first time Fuchida had stood before such a large crowd to speak openly about his Christian faith.

Fuchida told about his training as a Japanese Navy pilot and then as a loyal soldier of Japan leading the attack on Pearl Harbor. He spoke of his disillusionment at his country's defeat, and then he poured out his story, much as he had told it to Jake when they first met. He told of Peggy Covell and how her example had challenged him and his notion of *katakiuchi*. "Revenge has always been a major motif in Japanese thought. But I am here to say to you that forgiveness is a far greater moral than revenge," he said.

Fuchida concluded his talk by saying, "I know you long for peace—personal peace as well as world peace. And real peace comes only through Jesus Christ."

When he sat down, the crowd rose to their feet and cheered and applauded loudly. And when the applause finally died away, Glenn took over and invited those who wanted to become Christians to come to the front of the hall. Over five hundred people stood and made their way forward.

Jake was amazed. Throughout his year and a half of living and preaching in Japan, he had never seen such a large response of people wanting to give their lives to Christ. He felt that he was witnessing an extraordinary moment in Japanese history—a moment Jake firmly believed was the result of constant prayer for Japan and the Japanese people, by him and many Christians in North America and around the globe.

Chapter 17

The Ongoing Work

Spurred on by the success of the rally in Osaka, Jake and Kaneo Oda began an extensive evangelistic tour of Japan. Whenever he could, Mitsuo Fuchida joined them at speaking engagements. Larger crowds than ever before flocked to see the two opposing war heroes who were now united together in love for Christ. On the island of Kyushu, Jake spent a month preaching to coal miners. He conducted two meetings a day and spoke to an average of one thousand people at each meeting. As a result of Jake's speaking, up to four hundred miners a day stepped forward after the meetings for personal prayer.

When Jake returned home to Osaka to Florence and the two boys, he was pleased by all Florence had accomplished in his absence. The nightly Bible studies were bursting at the seams, and five members of Mr. Yoshiki's extended family had been converted to Christianity and now wanted to be baptized.

On Sunday, June 25, 1950, while eager and open Japanese audiences flocked to hear Jake speak at several church services, war descended on the Korean Peninsula. On that day an invasion force of heavily armed North Korean troops swept south in an attempt to capture South Korea and unite the two countries into a single, communist country. Americans in South Korea at the time were evacuated to Japan, and everyone waited to see what would happen next.

Two days later the United Nations Security Council passed a resolution calling for North Korea's immediate withdrawal from the south. If North Korea failed to comply immediately with the resolution, the Security Council authorized member states of the United Nations to act militarily against North Korea and drive their troops back to the 38th Parallel, the agreed-upon boundary established between the two Koreas at the end of World War II. When the North Koreans failed to comply with the resolution, President Harry Truman ordered American troops into South Korea as part of a UN force to help drive the North Koreans back. He put General Douglas MacArthur in charge of this operation. Soon an all-out war was raging on the Korean Peninsula.

Jake, like many in Japan, was greatly concerned about the war. If the UN force failed to achieve its objective, would Japan be the next country the communists set their sights on? Jake redoubled his evangelism efforts as he waited to see the outcome of the fighting in Korea.

In his monthly missionary newsletter home to the United States, Jake reported that he had preached forty sermons in the past month to a total of about sixty-five hundred people. He had given out six thousand Gospels of John and nearly twice that number of Christian tracts. As a result, over five thousand people had accepted Christ, and fourteen had been baptized. But, as Jake noted, plenty of work was still to be done in Japan.

As 1951 dawned, fighting still raged on the Korean Peninsula. In Japan, as the year rolled on, Jake and Florence busied themselves with their various ministry activities. They were particularly pleased with an ongoing youth outreach. At the end of July 1951, the two of them helped to arrange and teach at a youth conference in the fishing village of Yura, on Awaji Island. One hundred seventy young men and women gathered for the conference to pray, discuss their faith, and participate in worship services.

On September 8, 1951, in San Francisco, Japan signed a treaty that would have a profound effect on the country. It was known as the San Francisco Peace Treaty. Among other things, the treaty cut off Japanese claims to Korea, Formosa (Taiwan), Hong Kong, the Kuril Islands, the Pescadores, the Spratly Islands, Antarctica, and Sakhalin Island. It specified which surrounding islands Japan would control and exercise sovereignty over, authorized the carrying out of the sentences imposed upon those convicted of war crimes, and specified the amount of compensation Japan would pay to the countries it had invaded during the war. The San Francisco Peace Treaty would go into effect on April 28, 1952. The date would also mark the end of the Allied occupation of Japan and technically bring World War II to a close. From that date on, Japan would be a free and sovereign nation once again. Jake hoped and prayed hard that the country would indeed stay free and sovereign and not succumb to the advance of communism in the region.

Also in September 1951, as Japanese diplomats were signing the San Francisco Peace Treaty, calamity struck the DeShazer family. Just before his fourth birthday, Paul became ill and developed a high fever. When he started having convulsions, Jake and Florence raced him to the US Army hospital in Osaka. The doctor diagnosed his condition as encephalitis, a serious inflammation of the brain. Three doctors and several nurses worked hard to try to stabilize Paul's condition, but to no avail. Paul continued to get sicker and eventually slipped into a coma. At that stage a doctor informed Jake and Florence that they gave Paul a less than 50 percent chance of surviving. And if Paul did survive, he might suffer from brain damage or paralysis. Jake and Florence immediately began to pray that God would not let Paul die, and they asked the local Christians to pray with them.

Several days later Paul awoke from his coma and made a full recovery, with no lingering complications.

"It's a miracle," one of the nurses told Jake and Florence. "Your son has the worst case of encephalitis we have ever had, yet he has made the quickest and the most full recovery."

Jake and Florence knew that indeed it was a miracle. Their prayers and the prayers of many others had been answered, and they committed themselves to continuing their efforts to share the gospel with the Japanese people.

One of the things they threw their energy into was starting a church in Amami, a poor area in southern Osaka. A large storage room served as the church building where Jake preached each week as he won converts and built up the congregation.

As the DeShazers worked hard at establishing the church, Florence learned that she was expecting a third baby. Since she and Jake and the two boys barely fit into their current upstairs lodgings, the family decided that it was time for a move. They eventually moved into a new place near the Free Methodist Osaka Christian College. No sooner had they unpacked their things in the new home than Jake was off on a special mission: a summer evangelizing trip arranged to train seminary students from Osaka Christian College. Jake had three students assigned to him, and the team planned to travel to Shimizu and Tokyo to hold evangelistic meetings in both places.

Jake and the three students prayed together and prepared for their upcoming outreach. Then they set out for Shimizu, located 250 miles east of Osaka. They drove in Jake's car, on top of which they had attached two loudspeaker horns. Once they reached the city, they visited the mayor and explained their intention to hold evangelistic meetings in Shimizu. The mayor heartily endorsed their effort.

For the next five evenings, Jake would drive his car to the center of town and park outside city hall, where they would hold an outdoor meeting. One of the students played the accordion, another a pipe harmonica, and the third the cornet. The students provided the music for the meeting, interspersing the musical numbers with their testimonies. Jake would step up to the microphone, his voice booming through the speakers on top of the car, and tell his story of imprisonment and how God had changed his life. As Jake spoke, one of the students would translate for him. Though Jake was making progress learning the Japanese language, he did not yet feel confident enough to preach in Japanese. By the end of the five evening meetings, about four hundred people had shown up to hear the students and Jake, and ninety-nine of them had become Christians.

For the next five days, the team traveled into the countryside around Shimizu and held meetings in villages. Before they left Shimizu, Jake and his team had baptized seven converts and organized a Free Methodist Church in the city.

The team then headed for Tokyo, where they preached in churches twenty-five times and held six outdoor meetings. By the time they left Tokyo to head back to Osaka, Jake and his team had distributed over twenty thousand tracts and handed out over five thousand Gospels of John. As they drove back to Osaka, Jake and the students prayed and thanked God for the way He had gone before them and prepared many hearts to respond to the gospel.

In September 1952, a third son, Mark, was added to the DeShazer family. Jake stayed home long enough to make sure that mother and baby were doing well. When he was satisfied that they were, he set off again, this time on a preaching tour in Korea arranged by the US Air Force.

The air force sent a plane to Japan to pick up Jake and fly him to Korea. As he winged his way north toward Korea, Jake thought about how odd it was to be back in a military plane headed for a war zone. The last time he'd flown in a military plane headed for a war zone was nine and a half years before. Then he had been heading for Japan to drop bombs. Now he was headed from Japan to Korea to share the gospel with American airmen and native Koreans. What a strange turn his life had taken.

Once he arrived in Korea, Jake was kept busy. During the first week, he spoke at a number of Air Force chapel services, telling his story and challenging the men with the gospel. During the second week Jake was given special permission to travel to a number of restricted battlefront locations to talk to the soldiers.

The Korean War had been going on for over two years now. It had basically ground down to a stalemate along the 38th Parallel, the original agreed-upon border between North and South Korea. That did not mean, however, that all was quiet along the battlefront. Twice during his visit to the front, Jake had to scurry for cover in sandbag bunkers because of incoming enemy fire. When he wasn't avoiding enemy fire and conducting chapel services, Jake spent most of his time talking with or counseling airmen.

One of the highlights of Jake's trip to Korea occurred when he spoke at the Young Nak Presbyterian Church. The church had been built by North Koreans who had been forced to leave their old church and homes at the start of the war and had fled south. Inside the church a thousand people gathered to hear Jake speak through an interpreter. As he spoke, a chorus of amens would arise from the mostly Korean audience. Jake marveled at how different the Koreans were from the Japanese. The Koreans were much more demonstrative during church services than the normally reserved and polite Japanese. Jake found himself excited by the enthusiastic feedback.

As he flew back to Osaka, Jake thought over his trip to Korea. It had been a long time since he'd been among a crowd of Americans. He was surprised that they still recognized him and wanted him to recount his story of being part of the Doolittle Raid and his subsequent capture by the Japanese. This experience convinced Jake that he should accept the invitation to attend the next annual Doolittle Raiders reunion, to be held in San Diego in April 1953. He had not attended any of the previous reunions.

Jake traveled alone to the United States for the reunion. Florence was expecting another baby and could not make the trip. Besides, the whole DeShazer family was planning to return to the United States for furlough in the not-too-distant future.

At the reunion in San Diego, Jake thoroughly enjoyed himself. He had a great time catching up with many of his old Army Air Corps comrades, although a number of the surviving Raiders had stayed on in the military and were fighting in Korea. Jimmy Doolittle was there, larger than life. About halfway through the banquet, he whispered to Jake that a parcel had arrived for him in the lobby. Jake was puzzled for a moment, and then he nodded. Several weeks before, he had ordered five hundred Bible tracts to be delivered to him at the hotel where the reunion was being held. Now, in the middle of a banquet of five hundred people, the tracts had shown up. Five hundred people at the banquet and five hundred tracts—was it a coincidence? Jake didn't think so. He excused himself, retrieved the tracts, and began handing them out.

A waiter approached. "What are you doing, Sir?" he asked.

"Passing these out to everyone," Jake replied.

"But you can't do that!" the waiter exclaimed. "You are supposed to be one of the honored guests."

Jake shrugged his shoulders. "I want every single person in this room to get the message of salvation— they need to read this."

"I know that *you* can't give them out," the waiter said. "Here, give them to me. I will do it myself. You go back to your table."

Jake smiled to himself at the sight of the waiter offering everyone a tract as if it were a glass of wine. One way or another the gospel had gotten out!

In addition to attending the reunion, Jake was able to visit several churches while in the United States. In typical style he spoke at a large gathering at Greenville College, Illinois, and then enjoyed lunch with a Sunday school class who had saved their pennies all year to send money for shoes for the DeShazer children.

Jake returned to Japan ready to get back to his work preaching and teaching. He also threw his energy into supporting a Christian radio station. When funding for the station ran low, Jake and Florence agreed to use the last of his army back pay to keep it on the air.

Not long after Jake returned to Japan from the United States, the Korean War came to an end when an armistice between North and South Korea was signed on July 27, 1953. The armistice divided the Korean peninsula between North and South at the 38th Parallel, right where it had been divided before the war. Jake hoped that the armistice marked the end of the expansion of communism in East Asia.

Two and a half months later, on October 10, 1953, Florence gave birth to another child, this time a daughter, whom Florence and Jake named Carol Aiko (which means love in Japanese).

In April 1955, after six hectic years of living in Japan, it was time for the DeShazer family to return to the United States for furlough. Before leaving for home, Jake had one last task he felt compelled to complete. It was now ten years since World War II had ended, and many convicted Japanese war criminals were still imprisoned on death row awaiting execution. Jake's heart broke when he thought of their wasted lives, and he wrote to the American military authorities on their behalf. In the letter he pointed out how his own life had been spared: "I owe the emperor of Japan an eternal debt of gratitude. I would have spent eternity in hell if I had been executed at that time, for I was not a Christian." Then he added, "Our country was the first to drop the atomic bomb. Now let us be the first to show mercy."

Chapter 18

A New Strategy

In September 1955, Jake found himself once more behind a desk. This time he was attending Asbury Seminary in Wilmore, Kentucky, studying for his master's degree in divinity. The Free Methodist Church had agreed to continue Jake's salary and pay his expenses while he attended seminary. In exchange, Jake spent most weekends on the road speaking, sometimes with his family but mostly alone. His fame as a Doolittle Raider still drew large crowds of Christians and non-Christians alike. He loved to tell about his experiences as a missionary to Japan and about the openness of the Japanese people to the gospel.

Jake became even more popular in November 1956, when a thirty-minute television program titled *Return of a Bombardier* was broadcast on the ABC television network as part of the DuPont Theater Hour. Professional actors portrayed Jake's capture by the Japanese, his brutal treatment as their prisoner, his conversion to Christianity, and his going to Japan as a missionary.

It was a strange experience for Jake to watch someone else portray him on television and reenact events that were still vividly burned into his mind. Although he thought some of the scenes were a little overacted, Jake was pleased with the result. Anything that got the message of forgiveness out to the American people was fine with him.

The DeShazer children adjusted to life in the United States, though they were not always happy to be living so far away from what they knew. The younger children complained that American adults treated children more harshly than their Japanese counterparts, and the entire family struggled with leaving their shoes on indoors. However, the children did like many aspects of American life, including hot running water in the house and sports teams to join at school.

Jake's three years of study at Asbury Seminary in Kentucky passed quickly. Soon after Jake had graduated with his master's degree in divinity, Florence gave birth to another baby, a daughter, in September 1958. Jake and Florence named her Ruth. They were now the proud parents of five children.

While in the United States, Jake and Florence gave a lot of thought to how they could be best used as missionaries in Japan upon their return. Thirteen years had now passed since the end of World War II. In that time many Japanese people had adjusted their lives to the reality of a new Japan. They no longer felt the stark bewilderment of losing both the war and their veneration of the emperor. Those losses had led to a period of deep spiritual openness in the country. A foreign missionary like Jake could no longer expect to draw and captivate huge crowds at public meetings: it was time for him to move on to another strategy. The strategy Jake and Florence felt could now be the most useful in Japan was starting new churches, pastoring them for a couple of years until they had a solid base of converts, handing off leadership of the church to a local pastor, and then moving on to start another church.

Jake and Florence were delighted when the missions board of the Free Methodist Church not only accepted their strategy as a sound one but also allowed them to start their new endeavor in Nagoya—the city Jake and the crew of the *Bat* had bombed during the Doolittle Raid.

The DeShazer family spent Christmas with Jake's mother and stepfather. Hiram Andrus was now a stubborn old man of eighty-eight, and Jake's mother was still baking the best bread in the neighborhood at age seventy-five. With the prospect of four or five more years in Japan ahead of them, Jake was convinced that he was saying a final good-bye to his stepfather. On December 31, 1958, Jake, Florence, and their five children set sail for Japan from San Francisco aboard the MS *California Bear.*

Upon their arrival in Nagoya, the family found an American-style house in a section of the city called Smith Town. The area had been set aside to house American military families during the occupation of Japan. But now that the occupation was over, local families had moved into the houses. Florence was very happy with their new lodgings. For the first time since coming to live in Japan, they had running hot water in the house. This made washing Ruth's diapers much easier.

Once they had settled into their house, Jake and Florence did what they had always done before. They made friends with the neighbors, invited the local children in to hear Florence tell Bible stories illustrated with felt-o-gram figures, and offered English classes. Slowly they began to win converts and to fashion these new believers into a small but growing church.

Everything was going along well, when in September 1959 a typhoon slammed into central Japan. Jake and Florence lay in bed praying as the wind howled around the house. The electricity went off, and eventually, under the deluge of such heavy rain, the bedroom roof sprang a leak. Jake and Florence climbed out of bed and piled their mattress and clothing up against the most sheltered wall. Jake kicked himself for not being more prepared. All they had on hand was a small penlight, which they used to explore the rest of the house. The children were all sound asleep, and Florence decided that it was best to leave them that way.

Jake and Florence made their way into the kitchen just in time to hear a mighty swishing sound. Suddenly they were drenched with rain. The kitchen roof had been ripped off. Fortunately, the rest of the house stayed intact.

At first light Jake ventured outside to survey the damage. Many pine trees lay in the yard, their limbs poking out at odd angles, but none of them had penetrated the house. Many other houses in the street had not fared so well. Foundations protruded from the ground where once whole houses stood. The trunks of fallen trees crisscrossed the roads, and people wandered distractedly through roofless homes. Jake was amazed at some of the women who normally took good care of their appearance. Their hair was tangled, and some of them told Jake that they had spent the entire night screaming. "What did *your* wife do?" they asked Jake.

"We prayed together and trusted God to protect us," Jake replied.

"And what about the children? Surely they were very afraid."

Jake shook his head. "They slept right through the storm," he told them.

The women were amazed, and several of them became interested in the DeShazers' Bible study as a result of their calm faith under pressure.

In the aftermath of the typhoon, Jake and Florence had many other opportunities to speak of their faith. They had no running water for weeks, and washing the family's clothing in a nearby creek gave Florence the chance to get to know many of the neighborhood women better. When the community had difficulty getting electricity restored to their homes, Florence went with a delegation of local women to see what could be done about the situation.

By December 1963, the church was functioning well. New members were continuing to join, and Jake and Florence handed the leadership of the church over to a Japanese pastor. With their work in Nagoya done, it was time for the DeShazers to take another furlough back to the United States. By now Paul and John were both teenagers, Mark was eleven, Carol ten, and Ruth five years old. As Jake reflected on the family's time in Nagoya, he could not believe how quickly it had passed.

Once back in the United States, Jake and Florence made Salem, Oregon, their headquarters. Amazingly, Jake's mother and stepfather were still living and happy for the opportunity to get to know their five grandchildren better.

During the course of their furlough, Jake and Florence asked for a leave of absence from missionary work. They had originally left the United States with one toddler, but now they were responsible for five children. They both realized that the older children needed to attend American schools for a while so that they would be able to fit back into American culture and attend college or get jobs. They did not know how long this would keep them away from Japan but guessed that it would be between three and five years.

In Salem, Jake preached and taught as much as he could. He also bought a small farm to provide some family income, as the family did not know how long it would be before they returned to Japan. One year went by, and then two. Paul finished high school and enrolled at Seattle Pacific College. Meanwhile, the other children were fitting in at school. Ruth, who had spoken mainly Japanese, was now fluent in English and learning to read. John was a junior in high school. Mark had joined the church choir and the school basketball team, while Carol loved to sew and cook with her grandmother.

Finally, in June 1967, Jake, Florence, and the four younger children boarded a ship bound for Japan. Once again the family said a "final farewell" to Hiram and Hulda Andrus, who had just celebrated their fiftieth wedding anniversary. Paul stayed behind in the United States, as he was now in his second year at Seattle Pacific College.

Japan had developed much in the three and a half years the family was gone. A building boom had transformed the landscape, replacing single homes with multistory apartment buildings. Bicycles had given way to motorcars, many of them built in state-of-the-art Japanese factories. Attitudes toward foreigners had also changed. Japanese people no longer stared at the DeShazers as they once did, though Jake's clear, blue eyes still startled some children.

The Free Methodist Church in Japan was also growing, with new congregations being established around the country. And while the family had been away, Jake's faithful interpreter, Dr. Kaneo Oda, had died, leaving a large hole in the Free Methodist organization. One of the first things Jake and Florence did upon their return to Japan was to visit Kaneo Oda's widow and bring condolences from the Free Methodist Church in the United States.

This time, the mission board sent Jake and his family to live in the city of Hitachi, where a church already existed. Jake's job was to assist the pastor and to open up a new church in the nearby city of Katsuta. Jake met with a Christian family in Katsuta, and from there the nucleus of a church began. Jake went to work talking to the Christian family's neighbors, giving out literature, and preaching in the family's home on Sunday mornings. He also started a Bible class in English for boys on Thursday nights. The number of people attending the fledgling church began to grow steadily, and after only two years the Katsuta church had erected a building of its own and was ready for a Japanese pastor. Once again Jake and Florence's work was done, and it was time for them to move on.

By now John was nineteen years old and struggling to finish high school. He disliked studying and could not see much point to it. He was sure that as an American citizen he would be drafted into the military to serve in the Vietnam War. He left school before his final exams and headed back to the United States to enlist in the army. Paul wrote to say that he had finished his degree and had been accepted into the Air Force officer training program. Now Jake had two sons in the military. Though he did not agree with the Vietnam War, he knew that both boys would be called upon to fight in it.

The remaining five members of the DeShazer family then moved to Nishi Tokorozawa, just north of Tokyo. By now Jake had been appointed superintendent of the Eastern Conference of the Free Methodist Church in Japan. As a result, he had more responsibilities than ever.

In Nishi Tokorozawa Jake and Florence set about establishing another church, approaching the task following the same pattern they had used in Nagoya and Katsuta. But this time they were also able to work with two kindergartens and reach out to many young parents.

The new church grew at a steady rate, and at nearly sixty years of age, Jake continued to work hard to assure that everything went smoothly with the church. There was much to do, especially with the misunderstandings about the West that had been caused by the Vietnam War. Many Japanese people began to resent America's intrusion in Asia and had concluded that the Christian church was a part of a master plan to "win over Asia" to Western ways. Because of this, it was now harder to get people to listen to the gospel.

In 1972 Jake and Florence returned to the United States for another furlough, this time for just a year. They were especially grateful that they would be able to spend time with Jake's mother, as his stepfather, Hiram Andrus, had just died at the age of one hundred. Jake gave thanks for the godly and steady influence that his stepfather had exerted on his life over the years, and for the way Hiram had supported Jake's mother and provided a good home for her and four fatherless children.

By now all three DeShazer sons were in the military. Mark had been drafted into the army and was stationed in Germany. Paul was in the air force and stationed on the tiny Pacific island of Guam, from where US bomber aircraft were taking off to bomb Vietnam. John was in the thick of the fighting in Vietnam. Jake knew how brutal war could be, and he constantly prayed for his three sons, that they would have faith and courage.

The year at home in the United States was rewarding for Jake. He spoke in churches about the realities of war and how God had sustained him. He comforted many mothers and fathers who had lost their sons in the fighting in Vietnam or who lived in daily fear of a knock on the door delivering bad news of their son's death. And that was not all. Jake's alma mater, Seattle Pacific College, named him Alumnus of the Year in 1973, honoring him for devoting his life to preaching the love of God to the people of Japan.

Jake and Florence and their daughter Ruth were back in Japan by June of 1973. They immediately noticed that the mood of the country had turned ugly toward foreigners. However, because of his many years living among the Japanese people, Jake was still respected and loved by those he served.

Both Jake and Florence realized that this would be their last missionary term in Japan, and they made the most of every moment. Their family was all but grown up. The Vietnam War dragged on, and Paul was still in the air force overflying Vietnam in bombers. John and Mark had both completed two-year tours of duty in the army and were now safely back in the United States. Carol completed high school in Japan. She then went to Aldersgate College in Moose Jaw, Saskatchewan, Canada, where she met and fell in love with fellow student Ken Dixon.

Jake's mother died in 1973. She had lived to be ninety years old. A year later, in December 1974, Carol and Ken Dixon were married in Yokota, Japan. Jake proudly officiated at their wedding.

A year later a large Christian organization arrived from the United States to make a television special about Jake and Mitsuo Fuchida's lives. Rex Humbard and his World Wide Ministry spent a month listening to the men's stories and filming. At seventy-three years of age, Fuchida was ill and very weak, but still able to share his story and testimony. The end result was a book and documentary titled *From Pearl Harbor to the Pulpit*. The documentary aired thirty-four years to the day after Pearl Harbor on December 7, 1975. Jake was pleased to think that this was another opportunity to get the gospel out.

Captain Fuchida died May 30, 1976. Jake attended the Christian funeral, remembering his friend and brother in the Lord with joy and peace.

Before Jake and Florence departed from Japan in 1977, the couple spent the last few months visiting some of the twenty-three new churches that they had helped start during their tenure. Many of the churches existed as a direct result of the DeShazer's missionary efforts.

It was difficult for Jake to board the airplane for the trip home for the last time. He and Florence had invested twenty-nine years of their lives into the Japanese people, many of whom felt like family to them. Still, Jake knew that it was time to leave, and the opportunity to work more closely with the home missions board excited him. There was still plenty of work to be done!

Chapter 19

An Upturned Goblet

U pon their return to the United States, Jake and Florence were not yet ready to retire. They were both in good health and eager to continue their missionary work at home. For the first year they were back, they continued to serve under the direction of the Free Methodist Church, crisscrossing the United States and holding missionary meetings. The theme at these meetings was always the same. Crowds gathered to hear the story of the Doolittle Raider who returned to bless the country that had taken him captive and tortured him for forty months.

Those attending the meetings were different now, however. The World War II generation brought their children and grandchildren to catch a glimpse of history. Jake made sure that they got more than that!

Every person he preached to went home with a clear sense of the gospel.

After a year of constant travel, Jake and Florence settled back in Salem, Oregon. It was now 1978, and they had been gone from the United States for most of the past thirty years. They had ten grandchildren to get to know, and Jake also served as the assistant pastor at a local Free Methodist Church in Salem.

Now that they were home for good, Jake was able to consistently attend the Doolittle Raiders reunions each April. In April 1978 he made his way to Rapid City, South Dakota, for the reunion. About fifty members of the Doolittle Raiders were still alive, and Jake was among the oldest of them. George Barr had died of a heart attack in 1957, but Bob Hite and Jake still represented the crew of the *Bat* at the reunions. The two of them, along with Chase Neilson, were like family now, calling and writing to each other throughout the year. Jake was especially close to Bob, who had become an enthusiastic Christian later in life.

The Doolittle Raiders reunions evolved over the years from simply being a time for those who participated in the raid to get together and fellowship and reminisce to giving back to the community where the reunion was being held. In each of these cities, a talented young man or woman seeking a job in the aerospace industry was offered a college scholarship in the name of Jimmy Doolittle.

At the 1959 reunion held in Tucson, Arizona, the city presented the Doolittle Raiders with eighty silver goblets in a custom-made display case. Each goblet bore the name of one of the Raiders, inscribed the right way up on one side and inverted on the other side. The goblets bearing the names of dead Raiders were turned upside down, while the goblets representing those still alive were left right side up. At each Doolittle Raiders reunion, a roll call of those living was taken. Those in attendance answered for their comrades who were absent. Each man present then took his goblet and drank a toast to his comrades. The last two Doolittle Raiders left alive would eventually open a special bottle of vintage cognac and toast all of their departed comrades. Of course, when he attended the reunions, in keeping with his pledge, Jake would drink only water from his goblet, while the others toasted with cognac.

The 1994 reunion held in Fresno, California, was particularly poignant for everyone who attended, including Jake. General Jimmy Doolittle had died in September 1993, at the age of ninety-six. Right to the end of his life he referred to the Raiders as "his boys." Even in their own advanced years, the members of the Doolittle Raiders loved the title. Jimmy Doolittle had truly been a father figure to many of them, and now it was time for General Doolittle's goblet to also be turned upside down.

In 2001 Jake was visited by Mitsuo Fuchida's adult children, Miyako and Joe, at Jake's home in Salem. Jake recalled what a faithful friend and coworker their father had been and how he and Fuchida had sat together and reminisced on the last day they spent together in 1975.

Jake had, in fact, made three trips back to Japan since retiring as a missionary. Each trip he made had been at the request of the Free Methodist Church in Japan. While he was there, Jake would preach and participate in the celebration of various church anniversaries.

The year 2000 had ushered in the dawn of a new millennium, and Jake found it hard to believe how fast time was passing. Twenty-three years had elapsed since he and Florence had left Japan as missionaries. Jake tried to keep as active as he could in his ministry. Two years later, in 2002, Jake preached his last sermon at the age of ninety.

The next year, 2003, Jake attended the Doolittle Raiders reunion in Fairfield, California. It would be the last reunion he attended. Soon afterward he began showing advanced signs of Parkinson's disease. He also began to experience dementia. Slowly, Jake's world began to narrow until it became difficult for him to hold a conversation. Still, he enjoyed visits from his pastor, Doug Bailey.

On one visit Pastor Bailey asked Jake, "Do you remember when you were a prisoner of war in Japan?"

Jake looked quizzically at Florence. "Was I a prisoner of war?" he asked.

"Yes, Dear," she replied, "You were a prisoner of the Japanese for over three years."

"Oh," Jake said. "Really?"

Doug tried another tack. "Do you remember being a missionary in Japan?"

At this question Jake's eyes lit up. "Yes, yes," Jake said. "The whole family was over there. We began churches around the country. How I love the Japanese people!"

The pastor smiled. Jake had long since forgiven the Japanese, and now he appeared to have also altogether forgotten their brutal treatment of him. But Jake would never forget giving the best years of his life to live among the Japanese as their friend.

On March 15, 2008, Jacob DeShazer died quietly in his sleep at home in Salem, Oregon. He was ninety-five years old.

Jake's military burial service included 21 Airmen from McChord Air Force Base Honor Guard assisting with the 21 gun salute. A single bugler played Taps, and a B1-B Lancer from the 34th Bomb Squadron at Ellsworth Air Force Base in South Dakota flew over the ceremony. The US flag that draped Jacob's casket was folded and given to Florence. Then, family members laid seventy-five yellow roses on his casket while singing "When the Roll is Called Up Yonder."

A month later Florence went alone to the Doolittle Raiders reunion in Dallas, Texas. She watched silently as his goblet was turned upside down, never to be used again. She recalled how Jake had always asked for water in his goblet while the others drank cognac. Yes, Jake had been a unique man, unafraid to stand out in a crowd and stand up for what he knew to be true. He had taken forty terrible months of his life and turned them into a life of triumph over hatred and bitterness.

Bibliography

Cohen, Stan. *Destination Tokyo*. Missoula: Pictorial Histories Publishing Company, 1983.

From Vengeance to Forgiveness: Jake DeShazer's Extraordinary Journey. DVD-ROM. Grand Rapids: Discovery House Publishers, 2007.

Glines, Carroll V. *Four Came Home*. Pictorial Histories Publishing Company, 1981.

Glines, Carroll V. *The Doolittle Raid*. New York: Jove Books, 1990.

Hembree, Charles R. *From Pearl Harbor to the Pulpit*. Akron, OH: Rex Humbard World Wide Ministry, 1975.

Hoppes, Jonna Doolittle. *Calculated Risk: The Extraordinary Life of Jimmy Doolittle—Aviation Pioneer and World War II Hero*. Santa Monica: Santa Monica Press, 2005.

Nelson, Craig. *The First Heroes: The Extraordinary Story of the Doolittle Raid—America's First World War II Victory*. New York: Penguin Books, 2002.

Prange, Gordon W. *God's Samurai: Lead Pilot at Pearl Harbor*. With Donald M. Goldstein and Katherine V. Dillon. Washington D.C.: Brassey's (US), 1990.

Watson, C. Hoyt. *The Amazing Story of Sergeant Jacob DeShazer.* Carol Aiko DeShazer Dixon, 2002.

Additional material was drawn from the Marston Memorial Historical Center in Indianapolis, Indiana, and from personal interviews with Florence DeShazer in Salem, Oregon.

About the Authors

Janet and Geoff Benge are a husband and wife writing team with more than twenty years of writing experience. Janet is a former elementary school teacher. Geoff holds a degree in history. Originally from New Zealand, the Benges spent ten years serving with Youth With A Mission. They have two daughters, Laura and Shannon, and an adopted son, Lito. They make their home in the Orlando, Florida, area.